PROJECT LETTERS

A Collection of 215 Letters to
People I May or May Not Know

by

Austin James Robinson & Co.

Copyright © 2017 AJR PUB

www.austinjamesrobinson.org/pub

All rights reserved

Cover design by Christopher Sullivan

First published on May 25th, 2017

ISBN:
978-0-692-90216-5

Some names and characteristics of people, places, and things have been redacted to protect the privacy of the individuals involved.

No part of this book may be reproduced in any form or by any electronic or mechanical means including information storage and retrieval systems, without permission in writing from the publisher.

*TO EVERYONE I WROTE TO,
AND EVERYONE I DIDN'T*

CONTENTS

CREDITS	i
A	1
THE LETTERS	9
Z	232
NOW IT'S YOUR TURN	234
ABOUT THE AUTHOR	245

CREDITS

I would like to credit many people who made this project a reality. What started out as a joking status on Facebook turned into what you are reading right now. More than 250 people made this possible. Of especially high importance is Christopher Sullivan, who designed the cover and has supported my brand for years – oftentimes through the creation of my logos and graphics. Likewise, I would like to thank Chelsea Louise Taylor for being a major inspiration for why I write and why I publish.

Thank you.

A

Well, here we are. I jokingly posted a status with the sole intention of poking fun at individuals who go on the web and post things like "LMS for a TBH!" or whatever. In case you totally didn't understand what I just said, essentially I asked people to 'like' or 'react' to a status of mine on Facebook for a personalized 250-word note. Here, I'll just show you:

 Austin James Robinson
April 12 · 🌐 ▼

haha like this status and I'll write a 250-word double-spaced MLA-cited Microsoft Word 2010 document about what I like about you and email it to you

👍 Like   💬 Comment   ➤ Share

There it is – the status that sparked it all. A couple of things: 1). Forget that I said "MLA-cited" – I have no clue how I would even cite a memory with another human being. 2). The status originally had exactly 250 'likes' and 'reactions' – the increase in these are from people who

interacted with the status after I had already written the letters. And 3). You'll notice that there are not quite 250 letters contained in this book – after contacting every single person, I discovered that many of them either interacted with the status as a joke or felt that they did not want to put me through any more agony than they knew I was already going to experience.

Ah, the agony. It's true – this "joke" took me over 100 hours to complete. From messaging every single person to writing their letters to emailing their letters out to writing this book, etc., I can confidentially say I logged well over 100 hours. A lot of people said things like, "You must have a lot of time on your hands." This is a telltale sign of someone who does not intimately know me, for my hands can barely fit the concept of time. While I was writing these letters, I was training for my current job as a social worker, helping my cousin move, working on probably about 15 other projects, and going through some pretty heavy shit. But I digress. The fact of the matter is: I posted the status, I committed to the "joke," and I delivered these letters. And on top of that, I wrote this book.

Here are just some fun facts that I would like to include:
- There are a total of 217 letters filed away on my laptop, 215 of which made it into this book. That means two people did not want me to include my words to them.
- Each letter took me, on average, 15 minutes to write. I'm not even about to do the math on that, but let's just say that writing the letters was only half of the battle.
- This entire project (book included) took me one and a half months to complete. It took me about five weeks to complete the letters, and an additional week to finalize this book.
- I actually used Microsoft Word 2011; not 2010.

And, of course, there are many more "fun" things about this project that I experienced throughout the journey.

Now… why did I do this? That is a valid question. What kind of person just decides to spend an exuberant amount of time writing nice words to friends (and, in some cases, strangers) on the web? And what compels that person to then create a book documenting the entire process? Well, let me tell you a little bit about my stance on friendship. Friends are the celebrities of my reality. I do not – nor have I really ever, – quote, worship conventional celebrities. I find the entire idea of idolizing people on a screen mildly interesting at best. When I was in high school, I got a t-shirt made that said my best friend's name on it. I did so because I really appreciated them at the time, I wanted to showcase that I loved them, and I considered them a celebrity in my life. Since then, I have create at least a dozen more t-shirts filled with the names of best friends, family members, and even people who have just completely changed my life. It got to the point where I was choosing which 'name' t-shirt to wear based on how I wanted to feel that day. Did I want to do well on an exam and feel hella smart in my classes? I'd put on my 'Colten' t-shirt. Did I want to kick life in the face and own the world for the day? I'd put on my 'Kate' t-shirt. (Middle and last names are intentionally excluded here for privacy reasons.) I have more than a dozen t-shirts to choose from – all with a completely different personality and energy that I can channel whenever I pleased.

Then I began to realize that people are what matter the most in my life. I have always valued friendship above all else. The wellness of another human being oftentimes takes precedence over all else in my life. A good friend once told me, "If I had to choose between studying for an exam to be taken tomorrow or help a fellow human in some way that is substantial to their life, I will always choose the latter." I immediately made a shirt with his name on it. Philosophies such as these are what make life worth living to me. So over the course of reading these letters, I want you to keep this in mind: To love another person is to see the face of God.

Okay, now before we jump in, I'm going to provide an in-depth description of what this process was like for me. It started with the status, as we already know about. I waited about two days before I took to messaging every single person who interacted with it. As I previously said, that initial number was exactly 250, which meant I had to create a non-personalized chain text (which, by the way, people inherently hate and can sniff out with extreme ease). This was that message:

APR 14TH, 7:26PM

> Hi! You liked my status regarding me writing you a 250-word document stating what I like about you! What's your email (or any other form of communication you'd prefer me to use) so I can send you the document once finished? It might take about a month for delivery because I have a lot of them to do.

This took about three or four hours. Immediately, I knew I had signed myself up for a long journey. I compiled a list of names and email addresses in order of who interacted with the status first to last. Then I began to write the letters. I'll be honest: I took a very "college student" approach to this and wrote a couple of letters each week until I realized that these were going to take forever to write and I was closing up on the "month" I had promised everyone in my chain message, to which I then wrote the majority of them in the next two weeks.

On the next page, you'll find a sample letter to showcase the layout I used.

PROJECT LETTERS

Jason Thompson,

If you're reading this, it's because you 'liked' or 'reacted' to a Facebook status I made back in April. I know, it's been awhile and I suck! I expect you to expect me to send you the Cheesecake Factory Menu or something – and honestly I will do that at a later time if you wish, – but this is a letter containing things I appreciate about you.

1). How often you suggest new t-shirt ideas to me. I don't know if you remember this, but you have asked me to make a t-shirt at least two different times. You asked me to make one that says, "GO FUCK YOURSELF SAN DIEGO" and one that says, "JASON MUTHA FUCKIN' THOMPSON" – both very good ideas, and I apologize for never creating them. In my defense, the t-shirt shop I use does not allow cursing on their products (I know – they SUCK), so there was no way I was going to be able to make you those shirts. But someday!

2). The fact that you look fucking hot with both long hair and short hair. Yeah, you joined APO with long-ass hair and it was really cool and you were really cool. And you're still really cool! So I guess your personality isn't solely in your hair is what we've all learned here. Amen.

3). Anyway, wtf, we need to catch up and actually talk and update each other on lives and whatnot. I feel like we haven't *really* talked since, like, pledge semester back in 2014. Not that we've ever been great friends or anything, but I believe you did used to live, like, in the same building as me at Town Lake. What the heck!

Anyway, I really appreciate you a whole lot. I hope to get to know you even better from here on out! Seriously. Don't be afraid to contact me at the below information. xo.

Sincerely,
Austin James Robinson

I addressed the person, wrote a chain introduction (no one knows this yet, surprise!), addressed two to five reasons why I appreciate said person in bullet point format, closed it with a chain conclusion, and signed off. In the official letter, I also put "TO: [person's name], FROM: AUSTIN JAMES ROBINSON" in the header, provided an electronic signature, and stated my phone number and email address. Likewise, I put my website URL in the footer for shameless brand promotion. As you'll notice in the sample letter, which was used with Jason Thompson's expressed request, I have bolded the parts of the letter that are entirely personalized and unique. I know – I kind of cheated the 250-word rule by making 99 of those words non-personalized. But do you know how hard it is to sit down and write that many words about hundreds of people? I almost regretted not committing to just 100 words.

After the letters were finished, signed, proof-read, and converted to a PDF format, I emailed them out. Again, another task that seemed easy, but actually took more time than expected. I had to send this to 217 people, significantly less than the Facebook message I had to send. But you know what that means: another chain message. Below is verbatim what my email said:

Hi friend!

TLDR: Choose an option in the fourth paragraph.

As you know but may not remember, I created a post on Facebook back in mid-April that encouraged people to 'like' or 'react' to it in order to receive a 250-word letter of affirmation. You most likely interacted with the post because you deemed it funny or something no one would actually follow through with. Well, the entire point of this email is to prove you wrong. You may also think, "Wow, it's sweet, but… he has too much time on his hands." Again, you're wrong. But your friendship means something to me, and I'm not still breathing and living on this earth to take you for granted.

Attached you will find your letter. Yes, it is personalized. Yes, I sincerely wrote every bit of it. No, I will not be dispersing it on Facebook or posting it on your wall. But that does bring me to why your response to this email is highly recommended:

I want to make this into a book. I'll be honest, I made that post with comedic intentions and didn't expect for it to be 'liked' 250 times. A lot of people assumed I was either being funny, or that I would be the type of fool who would sincerely write every single letter. Well, the answer is both. And from my conversations with all of you regarding how to send this email, I had several people tell me they believe this would be an interesting and strong book to publish.

However, because of how personal these letters are, I obviously know I can't just publish it. So, I need to know whether or not I have your blessing and choice of three options:
1). I can include your letter inside the book with everything out in the open,
2). I can include your letter inside the book with important details (names, places, things, etc.) blacked out so that no one will know it was written to you, or
3). I cannot include your letter inside the book under any circumstance.

If you do not respond to this email with your choice, I will be utilizing #2. (Again, important details will be blacked out and there will be no way someone will know I am writing to you – I'll make damn sure of that.)

I am not looking to capitalize off of our friendship or violate your privacy whatsoever. Once I am done with the book, I will provide you a free PDF version. I will also not be marketing this book – its sole purpose will be for me (and whoever else wants it) to have a tangible item containing these letters, my thoughts about friendship, and my relationship with everyone involved. Opposed to being a social media experiment or a profit-making project, this is more of a sentimental showcase on the importance of friendship and caring.

Happy Monday, and thank you.

Thank God for the idea of chain messages because that email was longer than the average letter I sent. As I watched the responses pour in, I was actually quite surprised that so many people were willing to have our friendship details published.

And now I'm sitting here writing this book; my final step in this project that started out as a joke on Facebook.

Enjoy.

THE LETTERS

So here they are! The letters. As you will notice, they are in alphabetical order based on first names. Don't try to guess the [REDACTED] names though because they have been shuffled. Each one was carefully crafted and personalized to showcase either the memories of friendship I had with the person or something about their character that I intensely appreciate. You'll notice some personal stories, too – those are for when I absolutely did not truly know the person well enough to warrant a 250-word letter; however, I did not want to ignore their importance – albeit small – in my life, so they are included.

Aaron Dehn,

If you're reading this, it's because you 'liked' or 'reacted' to a Facebook status I made back in April. I know, it's been awhile and I suck! I expect you to expect me to send you the Cheesecake Factory Menu or something – and honestly I will do that at a later time if you wish, – but this is a letter containing things I appreciate about you.

1). Your dedication to Alpha Phi Omega. We met in APO and I really haven't seen you since I left APO (except I think at some random apartment party – but who can never be sure?), but I remember you being really popular in that organization and everyone truly loving you. I think maybe it was because of your personality, or your amazing looks, or because you're perfect? Idk – I guess we'll never know!

2). How good at photography you are. You are on GAME with that headshot / graduation photo Facebook 'like' page. All of the images are so beautiful and I love seeing my friends look flawless because of your photography. I hope this is something you end up doing forever and ever! Which I'm sure you will! Let me know if you ever need any help or anything! Not sure what I could do, but whatever!

Anyway, I really appreciate you a whole lot. I hope to get to know you even better from here on out! Seriously. Don't be afraid to contact me at the below information. xo.

Sincerely,
Austin James Robinson

Aashima Garg,

If you're reading this, it's because you 'liked' or 'reacted' to a Facebook status I made back in April. I know, it's been awhile and I suck! I expect you to expect me to send you the Cheesecake Factory Menu or something – and honestly I will do that at a later time if you wish, – but this is a letter containing things I appreciate about you.

1). How we used to see each other at Tejas Coffee Thursdays until I stopped going because I really only ever went to steal their orange soda (or whatever) and piss them off, then it stopped being fun. Sorry for totally leaving you like that! I wish I would have gone to more coffees while I was in university – maybe we could have been friends sooner!

2). How you bought my t-shirt!! I mean, so did a lot of other people, but you were the only one who bought one in the BELO building! Is that a reach? Am I trying to make this moment too special? Who can never be sure. Regardless, THANKS!!!

3). How you're in spirits! Which is basically super connected to Texas Blazers. So we're sort of like brother and sister, right? Forever.

Anyway, I really appreciate you a whole lot. I hope to get to know you even better from here on out! Seriously. Don't be afraid to contact me at the below information. xo.

Sincerely,
Austin James Robinson

[NAME REDACTED],

If you're reading this, it's because you 'liked' or 'reacted' to a Facebook status I made back in April. I know, it's been awhile and I suck! I expect you to expect me to send you the Cheesecake Factory Menu or something – and honestly I will do that at a later time if you wish, – but this is a letter containing things I appreciate about you.

1). The fact that we met in [REDACTED] foreverrrrr ago and are still friends, if only on the web! That's pretty cool! I love how an organization like [REDACTED] can foster friendship among so many different types of people.

2). How you make jewelry and totally rock at it! I love the stuff you make so much! I wish I enjoyed wearing jewelry so I could buy some of it. I'll definitely look at your Etsy page in the future for gift ideas for my mom and friends! It's so exciting when I see someone enjoying something and then making it into a business. Very entrepreneurial of you. Keep doing what you love and you will be successful. Who knows – maybe I'll see your jewelry and pieces in a major store one day! Can't wait for that!

Anyway, I really appreciate you a whole lot. I hope to get to know you even better from here on out! Seriously. Don't be afraid to contact me at the below information. xo.

Sincerely,
Austin James Robinson

[NAME REDACTED],

If you're reading this, it's because you 'liked' or 'reacted' to a Facebook status I made back in April. I know, it's been awhile and I suck! I expect you to expect me to send you the Cheesecake Factory Menu or something – and honestly I will do that at a later time if you wish, – but this is a letter containing things I appreciate about you.

1). You know I can't write just a 250-word document about you, right? Mr. [REDACTED], my unfortunate Soul Mate. I guess the first thing I'm appreciative of is the fact that you are so open with me and we have discussed some pretty heavy shit. I obviously won't get into anything here, but I'm just happy you are able to open up to me about anything.

2). How transparently ethical you are. I'm pretty sure you live every part of your life along the guidelines of ethics and morality – something I've tried to do basically since I learned about ethics. And you are always willing to talk with me about ethics and how, sometimes, the subject can literally become subjective. And how you call me out when you believe I'm doing something unethical (this has happened once, and it shook me).

3). How I've met your family before. Like, three different times. I guess they're going to have to love me if me, you, and your brother are going to be polygamists together.

4). How dedicated you are to serving others and helping the world. From going to [REDACTED] to [REDACTED] to everything you do for [REDACTED]: you are amazing. Never stop giving.

Anyway, I really appreciate you a whole lot. I hope to get to know you even better from here on out! Seriously. Don't be afraid to contact me at the below information. xo.

Sincerely,
Austin James Robinson

[NAME REDACTED],

If you're reading this, it's because you 'liked' or 'reacted' to a Facebook status I made back in April. I know, it's been awhile and I suck! I expect you to expect me to send you the Cheesecake Factory Menu or something – and honestly I will do that at a later time if you wish, – but this is a letter containing things I appreciate about you.

1). The times we spent in [REDACTED] together. Although I was very flakey with [REDACTED], me and you were pretty good friends inside and outside of the organization. I'm glad we remained friends past the organization. I can't say that about a lot of people, so thank you.

2). The fact that you're LITERALLY in a [REDACTED] music video. I love how [REDACTED] used to pull that up every single semester in order to show the new members that we have a famous member hahaha. You totally [REDACTED]

3). How me, you, and [REDACTED] all went to the Trail of Lights together and it was just the grandest time ever. I really miss that. I wish we all lived in the same city still so we could continue having adventures!

Anyway, I really appreciate you a whole lot. I hope to get to know you even better from here on out! Seriously. Don't be afraid to contact me at the below information. xo.

Sincerely,
Austin James Robinson

Alec Chi,

If you're reading this, it's because you 'liked' or 'reacted' to a Facebook status I made back in April. I know, it's been awhile and I suck! I expect you to expect me to send you the Cheesecake Factory Menu or something – and honestly I will do that at a later time if you wish, – but this is a letter containing things I appreciate about you.

1). Okay, I think the only time I've ever met you was when we went to Applebee's together with Patrick Golden and some other people. So, I guess the only thing I can really appreciate about you (besides your humor) is the fact that we shared a moment at a mediocre restaurant that I still consider one of the best American food places of all time. So, honestly, this letter is going better than all of the other ones I have written so far.

2). Do you want to hear about the time I sent a Texas Prisoner the LaVeyan Satanic Bible? Okay, so I volunteered at this Austin-based non-profit all throughout uni that sends free books and educational materials to prisoners. Well, I opened a letter there and the prisoner was ONLY requesting the 1966 Satanic Bible written by Anton LaVey. Wouldn't you know it – I had been carrying that EXACT book around with me in my glove box for the past two years! I bought it in eleventh grade to piss off my English teacher for making us read the Christian Bible, and I just didn't know what else to do with it! Anyway, I sent it to the prisoner, but I have no clue what happened after that. Oh well!

Anyway, I really appreciate you a whole lot. I hope to get to know you even better from here on out! Seriously. Don't be afraid to contact me at the below information. xo.

Sincerely,
Austin James Robinson

EDIT: According to the individual, we did not in fact meet at the great all-American restaurant Applebee's. We met at a gas station. This entire letter is a lie. Except for the Satanic part.

Alex Mutammara,

If you're reading this, it's because you 'liked' or 'reacted' to a Facebook status I made back in April. I know, it's been awhile and I suck! I expect you to expect me to send you the Cheesecake Factory Menu or something – and honestly I will do that at a later time if you wish, – but this is a letter containing things I appreciate about you.

1). How amazingly beautiful you are. Yep, I'm going straight for that. I totally adore talking with you, and I hate when you say someone's out of your league. If that's the case, then I'm, like, 20,000 leagues under the fucking sea. Now THAT'S a reference! Trust me: you're not out of anyone's league. Never forget that you have an amazing personality and you're also hella hot. And cool.

2). How we keep planning to hang out (/ questionably go on a date maybe), but it never happens. And this is totally my fault. I don't know how to live life, in general, so it's no surprise that I avoid all responsibilities! But someday! I would love to finally hang out with you eventually.

3). That time we met for the first time ever and then saw each other again the same day. Both times were kind of wild – I was giving you a free book and then I was just super drunk and probably making you feel uncomfortable! C'est La Vie!

Anyway, I really appreciate you a whole lot. I hope to get to know you even better from here on out! Seriously. Don't be afraid to contact me at the below information. xo.

Sincerely,
Austin James Robinson

[NAME REDACTED],

If you're reading this, it's because you 'liked' or 'reacted' to a Facebook status I made back in April. I know, it's been awhile and I suck! I expect you to expect me to send you the Cheesecake Factory Menu or something – and honestly I will do that at a later time if you wish, – but this is a letter containing things I appreciate about you.

1). How dedicated you were to mine and Daniel's weird ass Student Government Executive Alliance campaign. I honestly feel bad for exposing anyone to that, but you were all for it. I remember when you basically made a [REDACTED] about our campaign, dragging us. I believe it was satire, but you know, who can never be sure? We need more people to expose me like you did! Also, you were totally down to see our documentary. Well, correction: you DID see our documentary. And that was really cool. Keep being supportive!!

2). How smart you are and how much you write about what you do, and how I don't know anything you're saying because I'm not smart. You also post writings you've done about certain things like [REDACTED] and [REDACTED]. I see them on Facebook and [REDACTED], and they're very inspiring because it makes me want to write more about what matters opposed to just comedy.

Anyway, I really appreciate you a whole lot. I hope to get to know you even better from here on out! Seriously. Don't be afraid to contact me at the below information. xo.

Sincerely,
Austin James Robinson

Alexzandria Wagner,

If you're reading this, it's because you 'liked' or 'reacted' to a Facebook status I made back in April. I know, it's been awhile and I suck! I expect you to expect me to send you the Cheesecake Factory Menu or something – and honestly I will do that at a later time if you wish, – but this is a letter containing things I appreciate about you.

1). How I don't think we've ever met each other??? I really don't think we have, but this could be one of those moments where we have and I'm a piece of shit. It happens often. But if we haven't, I think that's hilarious and we should almost keep it that way. If we ever end up in the same place, we should pull something over our eyes and pretend we don't notice each other at all. It's the only way now.

2). How we were supposed to see La La Land together (for the second time for each of us), but then it didn't happen. So basically all of these "appreciation" points are about how we have never seen each other or we had plans and they didn't go through. Wow, I love us!

3). Your sense of humor. You're weird as fuck! We haven't personally talked much, but you have a great social presence, and everyone else seems to love your humor. Keep doing that.

Anyway, I really appreciate you a whole lot. I hope to get to know you even better from here on out! Seriously. Don't be afraid to contact me at the below information. xo.

Sincerely,
Austin James Robinson

Alicia Valdez,

If you're reading this, it's because you 'liked' or 'reacted' to a Facebook status I made back in April. I know, it's been awhile and I suck! I expect you to expect me to send you the Cheesecake Factory Menu or something – and honestly I will do that at a later time if you wish, – but this is a letter containing things I appreciate about you.

1). How bold you are with your activism. I have experienced you advocating and standing up for oppressed / marginalized / misrepresented / underprivileged communities both in person and online (IRL & URL). You don't care about what people think, as long as you know you are spreading the idea of equality and acceptance. I may not know as much as you and don't fight as hard as you, but you constantly inspire me to do more and learn, learn, learn. I hope to continue learning from you even after university!

2). How dedicated you were to the Kevin/Binna Student Government Executive Alliance campaign (and the administration afterwards). I met you while campaigning, and you were one of the reasons that I was continuously going over to the KB table even though I was campaigning for myself. You were one of reasons all of the campaigns were able to come together and have FUN while campaigning opposed to attacking each other or something. I am incredibly grateful for that

Anyway, I really appreciate you a whole lot. I hope to get to know you even better from here on out! Seriously. Don't be afraid to contact me at the below information. xo.

Sincerely,
Austin James Robinson

[NAME REDACTED],

If you're reading this, it's because you 'liked' or 'reacted' to a Facebook status I made back in April. I know, it's been awhile and I suck! I expect you to expect me to send you the Cheesecake Factory Menu or something – and honestly I will do that at a later time if you wish, – but this is a letter containing things I appreciate about you.

1). Hey! Okay, so you already know this, but we don't even really know each other! How can I appreciate you or write this letter if that's the case? Let's get to know each other and chat about things we might have in common! Or don't have in common! Let's fight! Let's become enemies! I'm down for whatever! Why do I keep using exclamation points! Anyway, until then, here's a story:

2). Okay, so one time I got to speak to Soulja Boy on Skype. You know, THE Soulja Boy. The one who was SUPPOSED to win the 2008 Grammy Award for the category of Best Rap Song. He essentially created the national anthem (Crank Dat), and we all severely underappreciated him. Anyway, I got to do a video call with him, and the only thing I could spit out was, "DUDE, YOU TOTALLY DESERVED THE 2008 GRAMMY FOR BEST RAP SONG" and he was just like, "Belee dat!" and then signed off. Anyway, now tell me your favorite story featuring Soulja Boy!

Anyway, I really appreciate you a whole lot. I hope to get to know you even better from here on out! Seriously. Don't be afraid to contact me at the below information. xo.

Sincerely,
Austin James Robinson

Andrea Martinez,

If you're reading this, it's because you 'liked' or 'reacted' to a Facebook status I made back in April. I know, it's been awhile and I suck! I expect you to expect me to send you the Cheesecake Factory Menu or something – and honestly I will do that at a later time if you wish, – but this is a letter containing things I appreciate about you.

1). How sweet you are. You are probably the sweetest person I've ever met. It was such an honor to be in your friend group while doing Study Abroad in England. I think we were all pretty kick-ass, but you were definitely the sweetest and most levelheaded person (even while some drama might have been happening). Even though you are a pretty quiet person, you are still nice and caring to everyone.

2). Your poetry. I remember you writing the most amazing poetry out of everyone in our course over at Oxford. Everyone was pretty shocked by it. I hope you're still writing poetry, and I hope you're putting it out there! You could really write a poetry book one day! I would offer to publish it for you, but I definitely think it could do well with a major publisher! (Unless poetry was just a one-time thing for you at Oxford and it actually doesn't make you happy – then definitely don't do it :P)

3). That time we sat on the bus together at UT while heading to the tennis courts. We talked about hang-out plans with Jay, which never happened. But it may someday! Probably not because now we're all graduating, but let's pretend it did!

Anyway, I really appreciate you a whole lot. I hope to get to know you even better from here on out! Seriously. Don't be afraid to contact me at the below information. xo.

Sincerely,
Austin James Robinson

PROJECT LETTERS

Anessa Sparks,

If you're reading this, it's because you 'liked' or 'reacted' to a Facebook status I made back in April. I know, it's been awhile and I suck! I expect you to expect me to send you the Cheesecake Factory Menu or something – and honestly I will do that at a later time if you wish, – but this is a letter containing things I appreciate about you.

1). We've known each other for years. I didn't go to Early, but most of my friends did and we definitely ran in the same circles. I guess we lost touch once I moved away for university and sort of left most of my hometown friends behind. But I'm really glad we've reconnected, even if it's just online. I remember you having an amazing personality and being a really caring individual. However, I guess I can't really write a good 250-word letter about what I appreciate about you considering we don't know each other much anymore. But here's a story about teenage girl fashion trends:

2). I'm not sure if this happened in Early or not, but do you remember when girls would wear their sequin belts around their boobs back in 5th grade? Was that just a thing at Brownwood? Maybe you were one of those girls! I mean, it was a LOOK. Literally the belts were made for the waist – as all belts are made for – but these teenage girls in the mid-2000s literally wore them across their boobs. Iconic.

Anyway, I really appreciate you a whole lot. I hope to get to know you even better from here on out! Seriously. Don't be afraid to contact me at the below information. xo.

Sincerely,
Austin James Robinson

Austin Ferguson,

If you're reading this, it's because you 'liked' or 'reacted' to a Facebook status I made back in April. I know, it's been awhile and I suck! I expect you to expect me to send you the Cheesecake Factory Menu or something – and honestly I will do that at a later time if you wish, – but this is a letter containing things I appreciate about you.

1). How dedicated you are to the Carillon (I actually had to Google to see if I was correct in the spelling, and I DID spell it correctly!). Not only did you do it the majority of your time at UT, but also now you're doing it someplace else! That's amazing, and I know you'll probably do it for the rest of your life. Your love for it is inspiring and I'm glad you found that.

2). The fact that we [REDACTED] in the [REDACTED]. Amazing. I have nothing else to say about that. We did it, and now I can say I did that. Not sure others will be as excited (or surprised, really) to hear about me doing that, though.

3). The fact that you tried Law School, and knew it wasn't for you so you got out and are doing what you love. It takes a lot of courage to simply drop something – in most cases, it sounds easy; however, I imagine it was incredibly hard for you. In many situations, I wish I would have had the courage to quit something for the sake of my happiness.

Anyway, I really appreciate you a whole lot. I hope to get to know you even better from here on out! Seriously. Don't be afraid to contact me at the below information. xo.

Sincerely,
Austin James Robinson

[NAME REDACTED],

If you're reading this, it's because you 'liked' or 'reacted' to a Facebook status I made back in April. I know, it's been awhile and I suck! I expect you to expect me to send you the Cheesecake Factory Menu or something – and honestly I will do that at a later time if you wish, – but this is a letter containing things I appreciate about you.

1). How dedicated you were to mine and Daniel's Student Government Executive Alliance campaign. Man, you had all of the profile pictures and cover photos and whatnot. We didn't have that many people supporting us, so it meant so much to me that people like you were there. And you went above and beyond. THANKS.

2). HOW YOU'RE IN THE [REDACTED]. What the HELL. What are you even going to study? You're gonna be like the guinea pig for the school! They're gonna pump you with diseases! You're gonna die!

3). You're hot AND funny. A hell of a combo. Slow down! We can't KEEP UP! (Also you've been to the Cheesecake Factory at least once.)

Anyway, I really appreciate you a whole lot. I hope to get to know you even better from here on out! Seriously. Don't be afraid to contact me at the below information. xo.

Sincerely,
Austin James Robinson

[NAME REDACTED],

If you're reading this, it's because you 'liked' or 'reacted' to a Facebook status I made back in April. I know, it's been awhile and I suck! I expect you to expect me to send you the Cheesecake Factory Menu or something – and honestly I will do that at a later time if you wish, – but this is a letter containing things I appreciate about you.

1). The fact that your Facebook states that you're apart of [REDACTED]. I'm not sure how true this is considering we don't know each other at all, but that'd be pretty cool if it's true because I love Soulja Boy *so much*. Regardless, I think we need to get to know each other more before I write you an entire page about what I appreciate about you. So, I'll fill up the rest of this letter with my thoughts on Graveyard Hierarchies.

2). Have you ever heard of someone being a graveyard president? Apparently every single graveyard has an organization behind it that elects someone to be the president and the vice president and the secretary, and yadda yadda. How weird is that? The dead people don't even have a say! And what exactly needs to be done at a graveyard that warrants an entire executive board? Surely this is something you can put on your résumé – how are you going to explain that to your prospective employers? And does this go under volunteer experience, or…? Anyway, I'm just looking for some answers

Anyway, I really appreciate you a whole lot. I hope to get to know you even better from here on out! Seriously. Don't be afraid to contact me at the below information. xo.

Sincerely,
Austin James Robinson

Austin Smith,

If you're reading this, it's because you 'liked' or 'reacted' to a Facebook status I made back in April. I know, it's been awhile and I suck! I expect you to expect me to send you the Cheesecake Factory Menu or something – and honestly I will do that at a later time if you wish, – but this is a letter containing things I appreciate about you.

1). The fact that we have the same name. It's no surprise that the only reason we are friends is because we have the same name and not because we met at a high school leadership seminar back in 2013. Throughout our time at the University of Texas at Us, I think we were the only two students in the entire student body with the unique name "Austin." Kind of brought us really close together. And I will never forget that.

2). When we (AKA you) created a fake UT organization dedicated to the Twitter account of the famous singer CHER. Remember when she tweeted at us and everyone was immediately like, "Shit, I should have joined." But we basically ended the entire organization directly after that because the whole mission was to get her to tweet at us. And we succeeded. Talk about dedication.

3). The fact that you helped me with my Student Government Executive Alliance campaign! Oh wait.

Anyway, I really appreciate you a whole lot. I hope to get to know you even better from here on out! Seriously. Don't be afraid to contact me at the below information. xo.

Sincerely,
Austin James Robinson

Ben Miller,

If you're reading this, it's because you 'liked' or 'reacted' to a Facebook status I made back in April. I know, it's been awhile and I suck! I expect you to expect me to send you the Cheesecake Factory Menu or something – and honestly I will do that at a later time if you wish, – but this is a letter containing things I appreciate about you.

1). The fact that you have extensive experience in the music industry through your work at radio stations and whatnot. Actually, I think that's all we've ever talked about when we were both in Alpha Phi Omega. I think I asked you way too many questions about all of it because I find it incredible. Keep doing it! Be a famous musician! Do whatever you want!

2). Also, on that note kind of, I appreciate how we met in APO. I mean, I was at the tail end of my time in that organization and you were just coming in, but I'm glad we at least got to meet each other! I hope you're still involved with it and making a difference in the world and all that jazz.

3). Your hair. Idk, I just like your hair.

Anyway, I really appreciate you a whole lot. I hope to get to know you even better from here on out! Seriously. Don't be afraid to contact me at the below information. xo.

Sincerely,
Austin James Robinson

Ben Reymond,

If you're reading this, it's because you 'liked' or 'reacted' to a Facebook status I made back in April. I know, it's been awhile and I suck! I expect you to expect me to send you the Cheesecake Factory Menu or something – and honestly I will do that at a later time if you wish, – but this is a letter containing things I appreciate about you.

1). That time in that one class we took (I honestly cannot remember the name of it or the professor or where or what or when or literally anything at all) when you saw that I was looking up PC Music stuff on the web. And then you told me you liked PC Music, which was quite a time because back then they were pretty not well known at all. And then I knew I finally had a PC Music friend (I have more now – but back then I think I literally knew zero people who liked them). Anyway, that was pretty cool and is probably the only reason why we're still friends to this day.

2). Your sense of humor. You're also probably one of my only friends who really understands and likes the "Laughapalooza" Facebook page and that style of comedy. Literally everyone just assumes I'm wigging out when I laugh at that stuff – no one thinks it's funny. So thanks for making me feel like I'm not just sitting in front of a screen and laughing at nothing.

3). You're from Delaware. Okay bye!

Anyway, I really appreciate you a whole lot. I hope to get to know you even better from here on out! Seriously. Don't be afraid to contact me at the below information. xo.

Sincerely,
Austin James Robinson

Bethany Harper,

If you're reading this, it's because you 'liked' or 'reacted' to a Facebook status I made back in April. I know, it's been awhile and I suck! I expect you to expect me to send you the Cheesecake Factory Menu or something – and honestly I will do that at a later time if you wish, – but this is a letter containing things I appreciate about you.

1). Okay, to be honest, we don't really know each other that well. Like, at all. I know you're dating Christian Córdova (iconic) and that you have an amazing personality. But that's really it ☹ So instead of faking an entire letter containing what I appreciate about you, here's a story about a town that has had a fire growing underneath it for the past, like, sixty years.

2). What?????? Yeah, exactly. There's this now-ghost town in Pennsylvania called Centralia, Pennsylvania. Back in the mid-1900s, the Pennsylvania state government discovered that there was a fire that sparked in the coal mine tunnels below one of their towns. They tried three different times and millions of dollars to put out the fire, with no avail. So everyone that lived in Centralia just had to leave and they completely destroyed the highway there. The fire is still there to this day and is now spreading to the nearby town of Byrnsville (appropriate). Honestly, what the f*ck? Anyway, we should go there sometime.

Anyway, I really appreciate you a whole lot. I hope to get to know you even better from here on out! Seriously. Don't be afraid to contact me at the below information. xo.

Sincerely,
Austin James Robinson

PROJECT LETTERS

Bijou Bentley,

If you're reading this, it's because you 'liked' or 'reacted' to a Facebook status I made back in April. I know, it's been awhile and I suck! I expect you to expect me to send you the Cheesecake Factory Menu or something – and honestly I will do that at a later time if you wish, – but this is a letter containing things I appreciate about you.

1). YOUR DRAG. Oh my god – you are SO GOOD. Your looks, your art, your outfits, your style, . . . I could go on and on. I'm surprised you even liked this status because I feel like you're a pretty popular drag queen. Anyway, KEEP DOING IT, but honestly IDK how you can go up from here. I'm excited to continue seeing your LOOKS.

2). The fact that you went to Drag Con recently and gave out stickers and all that jazz. That's so freaking cool. I went to the inaugural Austin International Drag Fest (the city of Austin – not me, although maybe I should randomly start my own drag festival) because I was living in Austin, but I have not been to Drag Con or anything. I hope to see you there one day!

3). How nice you are. I mean, it's no secret that the drag community is pretty dramatic and – at most times – just straight up rude. I remember when some queen was coming for you (honestly I cannot even remember their name) solely because your wig line was out of whack or some bullshit. And EVERYONE was defending you because of how nice you are; even on THEIR status. And you reacted to it very calmly. It was just refreshing to see a queen who is down to earth and full of love and no drama. Keep being amazing!

Anyway, I really appreciate you a whole lot. I hope to get to know you even better from here on out! Seriously. Don't be afraid to contact me at the below information. xo.

Sincerely,
Austin James Robinson

Bita Ghassemi,

If you're reading this, it's because you 'liked' or 'reacted' to a Facebook status I made back in April. I know, it's been awhile and I suck! I expect you to expect me to send you the Cheesecake Factory Menu or something – and honestly I will do that at a later time if you wish, – but this is a letter containing things I appreciate about you.

1). The fact that you're studying abroad in Germany right now! That's so freaking awesome. I've never even been there, so I'm incredibly jealous! I hope you make the most out of your experience there – Study Abroad was definitely one of my favorite things to do in life so far. Keep me updated on how it goes!

2). Okay, so I'm going to tell you a conspiracy theory that I made up to distract you from realizing that I don't have much else to say considering we never really talk. Did you know that Taylor Swift served in the 1989 Afghan Civil War? Whattt? I know, but just hear me out. You know how she has that album entitled 1989? (Wow, what a coincidental year, huh?) Anyway, her first single off of that album was Shake It Off. Shake what off, Taylor? The memories of war? I thought so. Not to mention she casually dropped that single the day before Veterans Day. Not so sly. Anyway, think about some of the titles of her other singles from that album. Bad Blood? Out Of The Woods? What the heck! She's almost TELLING us that she was involved in that war! Anyway, I'm just glad to be bringing the truth to the people.

Anyway, I really appreciate you a whole lot. I hope to get to know you even better from here on out! Seriously. Don't be afraid to contact me at the below information. xo.

Sincerely,
Austin James Robinson

[NAME REDACTED],

If you're reading this, it's because you 'liked' or 'reacted' to a Facebook status I made back in April. I know, it's been awhile and I suck! I expect you to expect me to send you the Cheesecake Factory Menu or something – and honestly I will do that at a later time if you wish, – but this is a letter containing things I appreciate about you.

1). So, first thing's first, here's a story: The only [REDACTED] I've ever known was this one guy who I almost made out with back in middle school – but he was straight and it was hella scandalous at that time. I'm pretty sure we were "wrestling" over a lollipop because none of that sounds homoerotic at all. Anyway, sorry this wasn't really about you.

2). I have no clue who you are. And I really appreciate that. Not that I don't *want* to know you – I just love the mystery of it all. How did we even meet? Are we just art people who added each other on Facebook because we have a ton of mutual friends? Was it the PC Music forums? Have we actually met in real life and now this is really awkward for me? I guess I'll never know!

3). You call me dad. And that's what I've always loved about you. Never stop doing that, please.

Anyway, I really appreciate you a whole lot. I hope to get to know you even better from here on out! Seriously. Don't be afraid to contact me at the below information. xo.

Sincerely,
Austin James Robinson

Brandon Corpus,

If you're reading this, it's because you 'liked' or 'reacted' to a Facebook status I made back in April. I know, it's been awhile and I suck! I expect you to expect me to send you the Cheesecake Factory Menu or something – and honestly I will do that at a later time if you wish, – but this is a letter containing things I appreciate about you.

1). That time you invited me to UNT's Alpha Phi Omega event (honestly, I cannot remember what it was called anymore, as I have been out of APO for quite some time). Everyone was so shook that someone outside of the division, or whatever, was there. And I think my club was like, "Wtf, Austin, what you doing?" Iconic. How did we even become friends? I literally cannot even remember, but I imagine it was because of APO.

2). Your dedication to HIV/AIDS awareness and safe sexual practices. In a world (or state, rather) filled with abstinence practices, you are doing great work with your continuous dedication to teaching everyone about safe sex. Keep it up!

3). How you treat your turtle like your child. Beautiful. He/She (I don't even know the gender of your turtle) is like your fur-baby, but your scale-baby or maybe shell-baby.

Anyway, I really appreciate you a whole lot. I hope to get to know you even better from here on out! Seriously. Don't be afraid to contact me at the below information. xo.

Sincerely,
Austin James Robinson

[NAME REDACTED],

If you're reading this, it's because you 'liked' or 'reacted' to a Facebook status I made back in April. I know, it's been awhile and I suck! I expect you to expect me to send you the Cheesecake Factory Menu or something – and honestly I will do that at a later time if you wish, – but this is a letter containing things I appreciate about you.

1). How I met you during my first year at university and we still (sort of) talk on social media. I remember that fateful day when you and [REDACTED] were dating and I was just sort of sitting on the ground while every other gay guy had a significant other with them. But I thought you were so funny. Okay, this sounds like I'm just hitting on you or saying that I had a thing for you. (Actually, now that I think about it, I think I did have a thing for you.) Anyway, this is all beside the point.

2). You telling me about how [REDACTED] serves breakfast and how to order it online so it's ready when I get there. That probably actually changed and saved my life. However, recently I went to a [REDACTED] (like, literally a couple days ago), and they didn't serve breakfast. However, they had "BREAKFAST" displayed on their big sign. So, honestly, that was traumatic. Now I'm just going on a tangent. THANKS FOR BEING A HERO.

3). The fact that you studied [REDACTED]. I know this is, like, the dumbest reason to appreciate you – but you know how much I love [REDACTED] and how hardcore I was about being friends with all of the [REDACTED] majors. Anyway, I hope you're doing something cool nowadays with that degree, and that you start the next [REDACTED] or save tons of live, or some shit.

Anyway, I really appreciate you a whole lot. I hope to get to know you even better from here on out! Seriously. Don't be afraid to contact me at the below information. xo.

Sincerely,
Austin James Robinson

[NAME REDACTED],

If you're reading this, it's because you 'liked' or 'reacted' to a Facebook status I made back in April. I know, it's been awhile and I suck! I expect you to expect me to send you the Cheesecake Factory Menu or something – and honestly I will do that at a later time if you wish, – but this is a letter containing things I appreciate about you.

1). The fact that you drive a [REDACTED]. That's the only one I've ever seen, and you're the only person I know who owns one. I think those were, like, THE car back in the mid-2000s. And I know how much you love [REDACTED], whose career was relevant back then. So, honestly, I admire how dedicated you are to that time period, is what I'm really getting at. Amen. This sounds like a drag, but I promise it isn't at all. Or is it?

2). How dedicated you are to politics and engineering. I guess you sort of have to be dedicated to engineering considering you work more than 40 hours a week at the [REDACTED]. But I just wish I had the brain for STEM fields, and so I'm constantly in awe that you're so good at what you do. As for politics, you were a freaking [REDACTED] back in 2008. Woah. I don't know anyone else who has ever even expressed becoming [REDACTED]. So, this is sort of like the whole [REDACTED] thing. Iconic.

3). The various cult movies you have shown me. I think it's really just [REDACTED] and [REDACTED]. Both were, like, AMAZING movies and I'm finding a hard time even getting other people to agree to watch them with me.

Anyway, I really appreciate you a whole lot. I hope to get to know you even better from here on out! Seriously. Don't be afraid to contact me at the below information. xo.

Sincerely,
Austin James Robinson

Brianna Mccutchen,

If you're reading this, it's because you 'liked' or 'reacted' to a Facebook status I made back in April. I know, it's been awhile and I suck! I expect you to expect me to send you the Cheesecake Factory Menu or something – and honestly I will do that at a later time if you wish, – but this is a letter containing things I appreciate about you.

1). How funny you are. I swear, you have got to be one of my most humorous Facebook friends. Your posts are absolutely ridiculous, and I love it when someone comments thinking you're serious. That's the best type of comedy – tricking other people. Anyway, CONTINUE BEING FUNNY.

2). The fact that you're so into that Avril Lavigne conspiracy theory. Are you into any other conspiracy theories? I would love to hear about your favorite ones. I've created a couple myself. And I'm constantly thinking of more. We should think of a conspiracy theory together. Like, we could legitimately do this and, like, make a blog about it and a shitty YouTube video. I feel like this is definitely our fate as friends. I don't think it gets better than this. I look forward to working with you.

Anyway, I really appreciate you a whole lot. I hope to get to know you even better from here on out! Seriously. Don't be afraid to contact me at the below information. xo.

Sincerely,
Austin James Robinson

Bruce McGaughey,

If you're reading this, it's because you 'liked' or 'reacted' to a Facebook status I made back in April. I know, it's been awhile and I suck! I expect you to expect me to send you the Cheesecake Factory Menu or something – and honestly I will do that at a later time if you wish, – but this is a letter containing things I appreciate about you.

1). The fact that you were in band in high school and I was sort of the band groupie for whatever reason. Do you remember that? I was just constantly around y'all and there was literally no reason for me to be. I don't even know what music is! Anyway, you were one of the coolest and funniest band nerds. However, I always remember being like, "Bruce McGAYhe? Haha gay" (as I'm sure literally everyone did) because I just thought 'gay' was the funniest word back then. I promise I didn't mean that in a malicious way.

2). Speaking of band, do you remember when I got kicked out of that band party (literally why was I there?) because I stripped my Halloween costume off at the climax of Party Rock Anthem by LMFAO? I remember the drum major at the time telling me that he thinks I am the first person to ever get kicked out of a band party.

3). The fact that you're in the Air Force! That's incredible and I have actually been looking into joining the Air Force. I hope you're enjoying it!

Anyway, I really appreciate you a whole lot. I hope to get to know you even better from here on out! Seriously. Don't be afraid to contact me at the below information. xo.

Sincerely,
Austin James Robinson

[NAME REDACTED],

If you're reading this, it's because you 'liked' or 'reacted' to a Facebook status I made back in April. I know, it's been awhile and I suck! I expect you to expect me to send you the Cheesecake Factory Menu or something – and honestly I will do that at a later time if you wish, – but this is a letter containing things I appreciate about you.

1). How we met, like, a full half a year to a year before you were even in [REDACTED]. Do you remember when I came up to say hi to [REDACTED] and you while y'all were eating lunch and then he introduced me to you? Nice. And then we totally had a class together, and you got into [REDACTED] during that semester, and that was pretty cool.

2). That time you came up to me and looked at my backpack and decided to scream, "IS THAT A STEPH CURRY BACKPACK??!" And that was the moment I discovered that I did, in fact, own a Steph Curry backpack. And who Steph Curry is. Now I ironically talk about how much I love Steph and the Golden State Warriors (but is it even ironic anymore?). Anyway, thank you for that.

Anyway, I really appreciate you a whole lot. I hope to get to know you even better from here on out! Seriously. Don't be afraid to contact me at the below information. xo.

Sincerely,
Austin James Robinson

Caleb Saucedo,

If you're reading this, it's because you 'liked' or 'reacted' to a Facebook status I made back in April. I know, it's been awhile and I suck! I expect you to expect me to send you the Cheesecake Factory Menu or something – and honestly I will do that at a later time if you wish, – but this is a letter containing things I appreciate about you.

1). Your personality. You are ALWAYS incredibly nice to me and every single person that you come into contact with. I know that we haven't really hung out many times, but every single time we have, you've just been sweet to me. I know you always tell me that we should hang out sometime, and I'm sorry I never took you up on that offer while in university, but let's try to from here on out!!! I really do want to hang out with you!

2). The fact that we met in Alpha Phi Omega. I feel like I met SO many people in APO – from around the University of Texas, the state of Texas, and the United States. Literally half of these letters are probably going to say this on them. But I'm so glad I got to keep good friends from the limited experience I had in APO. I hope that someday me and you will look back on how we both used to volunteer together years and years ago.

Anyway, I really appreciate you a whole lot. I hope to get to know you even better from here on out! Seriously. Don't be afraid to contact me at the below information. xo.

Sincerely,
Austin James Robinson

[NAME REDACTED],

If you're reading this, it's because you 'liked' or 'reacted' to a Facebook status I made back in April. I know, it's been awhile and I suck! I expect you to expect me to send you the Cheesecake Factory Menu or something – and honestly I will do that at a later time if you wish, – but this is a letter containing things I appreciate about you.

1). Okay, first of all, I find it so hilarious that I am writing this to you right now. Do you remember that time we were both standing outside of the [REDACTED] by the tennis courts? And you asked if you could borrow my phone in order to call your mom to come pick you up? And I guess you saw a message on my phone that essentially gave away the fact that I am gay? And then you told me that you knew, but you were, like, fucking cool about it and never told anyone? This is too many questions. Anyway, that happened and I always thought that was such an interesting story – and I never thought I'd be close to your [REDACTED] someday, but it's pretty cool now.

2). The fact that you're a [REDACTED] and hella creative. That's fucking fantastic. I know we come from a place where a lot of people aren't that creative and they don't chase after huge dreams, and blah blah blah. But you defy ALL of that. And what you do is really awesome. I really hope you release more and more art throughout life, and that you love every second of it.

3). That one time when I was over at your house and I was singing "Little Boxes" and you immediately knew it was from the show WEEDS and we basically bonded for the first time EVER thanks to a show about a white suburban mom pushing an illegal substance. Iconic.

Anyway, I really appreciate you a whole lot. I hope to get to know you even better from here on out! Seriously. Don't be afraid to contact me at the below information. xo.

Sincerely,
Austin James Robinson

Carolina Herrera,

If you're reading this, it's because you 'liked' or 'reacted' to a Facebook status I made back in April. I know, it's been awhile and I suck! I expect you to expect me to send you the Cheesecake Factory Menu or something – and honestly I will do that at a later time if you wish, – but this is a letter containing things I appreciate about you.

1). Hi Carolina. Okay, it's no secret that we really don't know each other, like, at all. Like, we had class together, exchanged a laugh or two, but do we really *know* each other? Although you did post a Sufjan Stevens song once, and that makes me feel closer to you than anything that I can think of. But, unfortunately, it means that I will not be able to fulfill a 250-word letter about what I appreciate about you. But I CAN tell you a story about how I'm, like, super close to knowing Sufjan.

2). So, I matched with this guy on a popular dating app a couple years back. We became friends and added each other on Facebook. One time I posted about Sufjan, and this guy tells me that he went to university at Hope College with Sufjan and that they were best friends. Of course I'm like, "Yeah me too thanks." But then I go over to his place and he totally shows me artwork and poetry that Sufjan legitimately did while in college. Can you believe that? If I get any of Sufjan's contact info, you'll be the first to know about it.

Anyway, I really appreciate you a whole lot. I hope to get to know you even better from here on out! Seriously. Don't be afraid to contact me at the below information. xo.

Sincerely,
Austin James Robinson

[NAME REDACTED],

If you're reading this, it's because you 'liked' or 'reacted' to a Facebook status I made back in April. I know, it's been awhile and I suck! I expect you to expect me to send you the Cheesecake Factory Menu or something – and honestly I will do that at a later time if you wish, – but this is a letter containing things I appreciate about you.

1). The fact that we met during [REDACTED] and adventured around the [REDACTED] together! What a time. I wish I could do it all over again. (I legitimately almost asked if I could do the [REDACTED] again, but felt that would probably be overkill.) Also, congrats on graduating recently! I'm sorry that we didn't really get to know each other after our [REDACTED] trip. That being said, instead of stalking your Facebook and attempting to pretend that I know you enough to write 250-words here, I'm just going to tell you a story!

2). There was this one time where I thought Australians were going to kidnap me. Which, like, would have sucked, but maybe it wouldn't have. You know? So, I was in Centralia, Pennsylvania (look it up – that's a completely separate story) when I ran into these Australian folk on the destroyed highway. They asked me if I was "Daniel" (who?). I told them no and kept walking. Later I found out both me and the Australian party were looking for the steam tunnels. So they told me to get in their car (which I did for no good reason whatsoever) and we would drive around the small ghost town looking for steam. While in the car, they kept making jokes about kidnapping me and keeping me hostage. Luckily I video recorded part of it and was let go. However, sometimes I wonder how different my life would be if I would have actually been kidnapped. Also, I just realized that this was

literally a month before we went on our [REDACTED] trip. So I guess I wouldn't be writing this right now if I would have been kidnapped. Huh.

Anyway, I really appreciate you a whole lot. I hope to get to know you even better from here on out! Seriously. Don't be afraid to contact me at the below information. xo.

Sincerely,
Austin James Robinson

PROJECT LETTERS

Chandler Forsythe,

If you're reading this, it's because you 'liked' or 'reacted' to a Facebook status I made back in April. I know, it's been awhile and I suck! I expect you to expect me to send you the Cheesecake Factory Menu or something – and honestly I will do that at a later time if you wish, – but this is a letter containing things I appreciate about you.

1). How weird yet civically minded you are. Like, those two things don't typically go together. I have a LOT of friends who are service-oriented and want to make the world a better place, and then I have a LOT of friends who listen to weird music and like art and being crazy. How'd you end up as both? Idk, but keep doing it OKAY.

2). Our discussions. Idk, I just feel like every time we talk, it's good and deep and sweaty. Okay maybe not that last word, but still. You are extremely easy to talk to and like. I think everyone I know who also knows you is in love with you (literally – I have had talks with mutual friends who have said they're in love with you). I guess you're doing something right.

3). You're hot. Enough to warrant this as one of my points of what I like about you. In addition, your personality is boner-inducing. And I'd put that on a Yelp review about you! ~Emotional Shawty 2002~ emoji emoji emoji

Anyway, I really appreciate you a whole lot. I hope to get to know you even better from here on out! Seriously. Don't be afraid to contact me at the below information. xo.

Sincerely,
Austin James Robinson

Chelsea Beggs,

If you're reading this, it's because you 'liked' or 'reacted' to a Facebook status I made back in April. I know, it's been awhile and I suck! I expect you to expect me to send you the Cheesecake Factory Menu or something – and honestly I will do that at a later time if you wish, – but this is a letter containing things I appreciate about you.

1). Your personality! CHELSEA, REMEMBER HIGH SCHOOL? YOU WERE SO COOL AND I LOVED EATING LUNCH WITH YOU! You were always so positive and willing to be friends with anyone and everyone! I'm pretty sure so many people loved you in school! And I got to go to your house a couple of times, and that was cool! Keep being amazing.

2). Your willingness to be different. I remember you always just being yourself. You didn't try to be anyone else except YOU. I always loved that about you and that is why we were such good friends! You were REAL. And I'm assuming you still are! Continue to just be yourself.

3). The fact that you will help others. I remember you being just willing to help me with any problem I had, and to be there for other people. That is such an amazing trait, and I hope you're still there for all of your friends. Not a lot of people have that personality trait!

Anyway, I really appreciate you a whole lot. I hope to get to know you even better from here on out! Seriously. Don't be afraid to contact me at the below information. xo.

Sincerely,
Austin James Robinson

PROJECT LETTERS

Chelsea Louise Taylor,

If you're reading this, it's because you 'liked' or 'reacted' to a Facebook status I made back in April. I know, it's been awhile and I suck! I expect you to expect me to send you the Cheesecake Factory Menu or something – and honestly I will do that at a later time if you wish, – but this is a letter containing things I appreciate about you.

1). How you were homeschooled because your parents said that the Bible "says to teach your own kids" – like, that most likely really sucked for you at most times, but I think it's honestly the only reason we even became best friends. I remember coming over to your house after school a lot and you just being like, "Yeah I worked on English for, like, two hours today and now I've just been decorating my room." You also had the absolute coolest projects going on that being homeschooled allowed you to complete.

2). How free you are. You've always been taken away by certain music and places, and it allows you to feel like you can do anything. If you want to write a book or paint something or take a trip somewhere, you always do it. You don't allow the world to be concrete on you and place you in one place. I think you could really do some cool things in the future with your freedom.

3). How funny you are. We've had SO many inside jokes. And they're not just those "oh haha best friend" inside jokes – like, they're actually funny af and everyone would laugh at them if we got on a stage. Let's keep collaborating!

Anyway, I really appreciate you a whole lot. I hope to get to know you even better from here on out! Seriously. Don't be afraid to contact me at the below information. xo.

Sincerely,
Austin James Robinson

[NAME REDACTED],

If you're reading this, it's because you 'liked' or 'reacted' to a Facebook status I made back in April. I know, it's been awhile and I suck! I expect you to expect me to send you the Cheesecake Factory Menu or something – and honestly I will do that at a later time if you wish, – but this is a letter containing things I appreciate about you.

1). Your sense of humor. And I don't mean a typical "oh haha you're funny and you really *get it*" kind of sense – I mean, you are probably the sole person in my life who is not pursuing comedy but SHOULD. And, I mean, we've discussed this before, so this isn't coming as a surprise to you and you're probably yawning right now, but seriously. I'm not sure how I could help in any way, but I will figure out how to ensure you become a famous comedian in NYC or LA or WHEREVER.

2). How dedicated you are to [REDACTED], but also how willing you are to talk shit about them with me (in a good way, we totally mean well – of course). They're a great group, but there's a reason a lot of people don't really like them, lmao. In that same sense, there's a reason they're so strong and get shit done and have their name solidified around campus. And you stick with them throughout all of it. Iconic.

3). The fact that you call me drunk, like, all of the time. That's all.

Anyway, I really appreciate you a whole lot. I hope to get to know you even better from here on out! Seriously. Don't be afraid to contact me at the below information. xo.

Sincerely,
Austin James Robinson

Cheyenne Marie,

If you're reading this, it's because you 'liked' or 'reacted' to a Facebook status I made back in April. I know, it's been awhile and I suck! I expect you to expect me to send you the Cheesecake Factory Menu or something – and honestly I will do that at a later time if you wish, – but this is a letter containing things I appreciate about you.

1). How we've known each other for, like, probably a decade at this point! I remember meeting you in middle school and having a ton of mutual friends with you! It's no surprise that we eventually became friends and are still friends to this day! I hope to hang out with you again someday soon.

2). How dedicated you have been to my brand and comedy. You owned the shirt, you signed up for the newsletter, yadda yadda yadda. You've always been one of the people who love what I do and will support me no matter what. And that means so much to me. Thank you!

3). The fact that you're a mom! Okay, so I'm actually writing this on Mother's Day, but besides that, I have great respect for moms and raising children in general. Continue to love and advocate for your daughter! Make her one of the best human beings the earth has.

Anyway, I really appreciate you a whole lot. I hope to get to know you even better from here on out! Seriously. Don't be afraid to contact me at the below information. xo.

Sincerely,
Austin James Robinson

[NAME REDACTED],

If you're reading this, it's because you 'liked' or 'reacted' to a Facebook status I made back in April. I know, it's been awhile and I suck! I expect you to expect me to send you the Cheesecake Factory Menu or something – and honestly I will do that at a later time if you wish, – but this is a letter containing things I appreciate about you.

1). The fact that I can't remember how we met, but I'm pretty sure it was on a dating app. And how regardless of that, we still haven't met in person, but we've talked a lot and I think we have a road trip planned? Who can never be sure. Maybe we'll never meet IRL, but all we need is URL <3

2). Your sense of humor. Dude, your old YouTube videos are funny – and all of your [REDACTED] are literally so hilarious. And I don't even think you try to be funny, you just naturally are. ONE HUNDRED.

3). The fact that you moved to [REDACTED] right after I left! Iconic. You did that on purpose, and I love you for that. But seriously, I'm glad you moved to [REDACTED] and are having a lot of fun there! I see all of the adventures you are having (AKA finding a job), and I hope that you make the most out of living there (because God knows I didn't). I'll visit you soon.

Anyway, I really appreciate you a whole lot. I hope to get to know you even better from here on out! Seriously. Don't be afraid to contact me at the below information. xo.

Sincerely,
Austin James Robinson

Chris Yeates,

If you're reading this, it's because you 'liked' or 'reacted' to a Facebook status I made back in April. I know, it's been awhile and I suck! I expect you to expect me to send you the Cheesecake Factory Menu or something – and honestly I will do that at a later time if you wish, – but this is a letter containing things I appreciate about you.

1). How dedicated to McCombs and the Business Honors Program you are. And I think you might be apart of the Business Council? Or maybe I'm literally getting ALL of those confused because I don't even know what a McCombs is. Although, did I ever tell you that I did attempt to do that Business Seminar Institute and dropped out in the middle of the summer to live in LA for the rest of it? That's as close as I got to BHP. Anyway, this is about you. You're really dedicated to the BUSINESS. And that's really cool.

2). Kevin / Binna??

3). How you and my father have the same first and middle name. Christopher Alan. Isn't that just so awesome? Doesn't that make you want to be my friend even more? Do you feel closer to me yet?

Anyway, I really appreciate you a whole lot. I hope to get to know you even better from here on out! Seriously. Don't be afraid to contact me at the below information. xo.

Sincerely,
Austin James Robinson

Christina Marie Boatman,

If you're reading this, it's because you 'liked' or 'reacted' to a Facebook status I made back in April. I know, it's been awhile and I suck! I expect you to expect me to send you the Cheesecake Factory Menu or something – and honestly I will do that at a later time if you wish, – but this is a letter containing things I appreciate about you.

1). Wtf, what don't I appreciate about you?? Oh, what if I just wrote you a diss letter? Lmao, it's tempting but I'm not going to do that. Anyway, I guess the first and foremost thing I appreciate about you is the fact that we are the same exact person. Enough said. Also our lives align perfectly every time? It's so weird. We're gonna have to remain friends until we die to see if this keeps happening. Sorry! I don't make the rules!

2). Your free personality and how you do what the fuck you want. From your hair to how you conduct yourself, you truly live life for YOU and do not care what other people think. That's amazing and I can learn a thing or two from you (even if it seems like I'm the same way most of the time). If anybody ever judges you for anything you do, just remember that they aren't living your life and honestly, wtf, why do they care??? Whatever, you're FAMOUS.

3). How you're completely dedicating your life to service, through and through. APO, Youth & Community Studies, how you treat your friends – you truly give yourself to everyone all of the time, and that's admirable. Remember to be there for yourself, too.

Anyway, I really appreciate you a whole lot. I hope to get to know you even better from here on out! Seriously. Don't be afraid to contact me at the below information. xo.

Sincerely,
Austin James Robinson

[NAME REDACTED],

If you're reading this, it's because you 'liked' or 'reacted' to a Facebook status I made back in April. I know, it's been awhile and I suck! I expect you to expect me to send you the Cheesecake Factory Menu or something – and honestly I will do that at a later time if you wish, – but this is a letter containing things I appreciate about you.

1). **The fact that we met at a [REDACTED] seminar! I just always appreciate when I make a friendship at those seminars – and typically the people I meet and befriend at them are OUTSTANDING. You're no exception. We just need to update each other on our lives because it has been forever!**

2). **The fact that the first message I ever sent you is [REDACTED]'s advertisement for her run for International President at the Key Club International Convention back in, like, 2012. I don't remember the context, but I'm assuming you were also in Key Club or at least know who [REDACTED] is. Iconic.**

3). **How dedicated you are to service. I'll admit: I stalked your Facebook. And DAMN. You do everything. [REDACTED], [REDACTED], [REDACTED], etc. You seem like quite the exceptional individual – I cannot wait to see how you change the world one day.**

Anyway, I really appreciate you a whole lot. I hope to get to know you even better from here on out! Seriously. Don't be afraid to contact me at the below information. xo.

Sincerely,
Austin James Robinson

[NAME REDACTED],

If you're reading this, it's because you 'liked' or 'reacted' to a Facebook status I made back in April. I know, it's been awhile and I suck! I expect you to expect me to send you the Cheesecake Factory Menu or something – and honestly I will do that at a later time if you wish, – but this is a letter containing things I appreciate about you.

1). How dedicated you are to [REDACTED]. I know that I was leaving [REDACTED] when you were coming in, but I remember you being one of the most charismatic members to come into [REDACTED]. Likewise, you actually cared about the service and wanted to give your all into volunteering with the organization. I wish we could have been in [REDACTED] at the same time, but I'm still glad I met you and that you're doing so well inside of the org!

2). The fact that you applied to be in the [REDACTED]! At least, you went to a lot of the events and told me you were applying – I have no clue if you ended up applying. If you did, just keep applying because you would be a perfect fit. If you didn't, you need to apply!!

Anyway, I really appreciate you a whole lot. I hope to get to know you even better from here on out! Seriously. Don't be afraid to contact me at the below information. xo.

Sincerely,
Austin James Robinson

PROJECT LETTERS

Christopher Sullivan,

If you're reading this, it's because you 'liked' or 'reacted' to a Facebook status I made back in April. I know, it's been awhile and I suck! I expect you to expect me to send you the Cheesecake Factory Menu or something – and honestly I will do that at a later time if you wish, – but this is a letter containing things I appreciate about you.

1). Your ability to talk with anyone and make a friend out of them. I'm pretty sure most of our mutual friends are people who you literally met on the World Wide Web. And that's, like, fucking amazing. That ability is what's going to ensure you have amazing and creative people in your life all throughout it. Thank God for the web, am I right?

2). Your willingness to help all of your friends out. I'm pretty sure I don't know anyone else in my life who would allow me to stay in their living space – let alone their own bed – for a whole month. Like, damn. That was pretty awesome. And that's what I really needed at that point with everything that was happening. And I know you would do this for literally anyone else in your life, and that's amazing.

3). Your graphic design skills. You're basically the only graphic designer friend I have and it's so cool to be able to see your work and work with you creatively. I would absolutely love to be able to be a graphic designer someday – even if it is just a hobby. For now I'll stick with Microsoft Word, but you definitely inspire me to go further.

Anyway, I really appreciate you a whole lot. I hope to get to know you even better from here on out! Seriously. Don't be afraid to contact me at the below information. xo.

Sincerely,
Austin James Robinson

Christopher [REDACTED],

If you're reading this, it's because you 'liked' or 'reacted' to a Facebook status I made back in April. I know, it's been awhile and I suck! I expect you to expect me to send you the Cheesecake Factory Menu or something – and honestly I will do that at a later time if you wish, – but this is a letter containing things I appreciate about you.

1). The fact that we met on a dating app forever ago (like, years) and we have not talked to each other ONCE since then and yet, here I am: writing you a letter. Somehow I wonder how I even kept friends on Facebook when I really don't know them at all. I guess my brand is working! But seriously, I'm sure we both see each other's stuff on our timelines, so I'm glad we're still friends, regardless!

2). You're hot! Yeah, this is a shallow and simple one. I mean, you're pretty VERY attractive. That's always cool and good. And honestly at this point, I'm just trying to fill in things to make this letter longer because, like I said earlier, we really haven't talked much. And there's only so much I can say about you being attractive, and by now I'm really just extinguishing the fire that was how beautiful this letter was supposed to be, and probably ruining the entire experience for you. I am so sorry about that. Oh, good, okay, the word limit has been reached. MESSAGE ME.

Anyway, I really appreciate you a whole lot. I hope to get to know you even better from here on out! Seriously. Don't be afraid to contact me at the below information. xo.

Sincerely,
Austin James Robinson

Claire Orton,

If you're reading this, it's because you 'liked' or 'reacted' to a Facebook status I made back in April. I know, it's been awhile and I suck! I expect you to expect me to send you the Cheesecake Factory Menu or something – and honestly I will do that at a later time if you wish, – but this is a letter containing things I appreciate about you.

1). The fact that we connected while you were working on an opposite Student Government Executive Alliance campaign. Iconic. Literally I remember exactly where I was on West Mall when you came stumbling (almost literally) up to me saying, "Are you Austin James Robinson?!?" before continuing to talk about how you had been stalking my social media and brand. Amazing.

2). When me, you, and David went to The Cheesecake Factory and all talked about Black Mirror (AKA the perfect combination of all things). I'm pretty sure we could have made a talk-show called "David, Claire, and Austin at The Cheesecake Factory talking about Black Mirror" on Texas Student Television and it would have been the most watched show. Okay, let's actually do this.

3). COATS ON A BOAT. Remember when we won best couple at COAB? Well, technically that wasn't a competition, but whatever – we won anyway. Would we have been a power couple if we would have dated?? OMG

Anyway, I really appreciate you a whole lot. I hope to get to know you even better from here on out! Seriously. Don't be afraid to contact me at the below information. xo.

Sincerely,
Austin James Robinson

[NAME REDACTED],

If you're reading this, it's because you 'liked' or 'reacted' to a Facebook status I made back in April. I know, it's been awhile and I suck! I expect you to expect me to send you the Cheesecake Factory Menu or something – and honestly I will do that at a later time if you wish, – but this is a letter containing things I appreciate about you.

1). How I'm totally not sure how we originally met, but I'm pretty sure it's because you were a [REDACTED] major and I just added all of y'all. But what blossomed from that is a pretty great friendship! I have learned so much from you and your posts. You have definitely become one of my favorite Facebook friends, and I hope we get to hang out more IRL in the future!

2). Your constant activism. It's a great fight – one I need to work better on. You care *so much* and are willing to put everything out there to fight for intersectional equality, and we need people to be more open about that more than ever. You inspire me, and I admire you and your Facebook so much.

3). The time you totally let me spend the night at your apartment in [REDACTED] for almost a full week. And not only that, but you let two other people stay there, as well. And not only that, but you gave us a TOUR of [REDACTED] from a local's point of view. You are truly an incredible individual, and more people should strive to be like you. Thank you for everything. I hope I can repay you someday, and just let me know if you need anything!

Anyway, I really appreciate you a whole lot. I hope to get to know you even better from here on out! Seriously. Don't be afraid to contact me at the below information. xo.

Sincerely,
Austin James Robinson

[NAME REDACTED],

If you're reading this, it's because you 'liked' or 'reacted' to a Facebook status I made back in April. I know, it's been awhile and I suck! I expect you to expect me to send you the Cheesecake Factory Menu or something – and honestly I will do that at a later time if you wish, – but this is a letter containing things I appreciate about you.

1). The fact that you were best friends with Sufjan Stevens in college. I love hearing about all of your stories with him. And all of the artwork that you've shown me that he made. And the poetry! And when we made those plans to read Sufjan's hidden college poetry while naked. That would have been an intense date. Anyway, it's just so awesome that you have such a connection with one of the world's biggest musicians. Let's go to one of his concerts someday!

2). That time we ate at [REDACTED] and I not only left my credit card at the restaurant, but I also left my wallet in your car when all you did was drive me to my car in the parking lot. And I had to drive all the way across [REDACTED] to you in the early, early morning in order to retrieve it. But more so: I appreciate you for what you told me during that dinner. You told me about your plans to create an organization dedicated to ensuring the gay community feels at one and is getting the resources it needs. I love that, and keep doing it. It will become a reality one day.

Anyway, I really appreciate you a whole lot. I hope to get to know you even better from here on out! Seriously. Don't be afraid to contact me at the below information. xo.

Sincerely,
Austin James Robinson

Clift Anthony,

If you're reading this, it's because you 'liked' or 'reacted' to a Facebook status I made back in April. I know, it's been awhile and I suck! I expect you to expect me to send you the Cheesecake Factory Menu or something – and honestly I will do that at a later time if you wish, – but this is a letter containing things I appreciate about you.

1). How perfectly great you are at being yourself and not giving a fuck about what other people think. You and your art and everything you stand for are incredible, and I adore being connected with you on Facebook. I look forward to seeing your future content!

2). The fact that your music is really good, and that your art is incredible and I will never be able to do it. I'm pissed AND jealous! But keep doing it because I love both of those things.

3). Okay, so we obviously don't know each other *that* well, so the rest of this letter is going to be me telling you about the conspiracy theory I made up about how Florida isn't real. Do you even want to hear about this bullshit? Good. So, you know how no matter where you go, there's Florida license plates everywhere? Where the fuck do they think they're going? No one is taking up more space in every state besides their own except them! Did that sentence even make sense? Anyway, Disney World is a green screen, politicians who claim they're from Florida are lying, and your grandmother is definitely not in Florida.

Anyway, I really appreciate you a whole lot. I hope to get to know you even better from here on out! Seriously. Don't be afraid to contact me at the below information. xo.

Sincerely,
Austin James Robinson

Collin Acock,

If you're reading this, it's because you 'liked' or 'reacted' to a Facebook status I made back in April. I know, it's been awhile and I suck! I expect you to expect me to send you the Cheesecake Factory Menu or something – and honestly I will do that at a later time if you wish, – but this is a letter containing things I appreciate about you.

1). The fact that we met at HOBY once because of [REDACTED] and are still friends on Facebook! I know we probably have not talked since then, but it's fun to see you on social media and be like, "Oh hey – I met him at this volunteering thing a couple years ago and look what he's up to." LMAO.

2). Okay I just looked back at our message history and I guess I met you, like, a whileeeeeeee back. Apparently you told me about Alpha Phi Omega! And I ended up joining because you told me about it. That's so crazy because I could hardly remember what made me join. I ended up being in it for up to two years or so. Not only that, but I became the person who served the most volunteer hours in the entire nation for three semesters in a row. So, I guess THANK YOU! I wasn't in it for the tail end of my college career, but I definitely loved it so much. You'll have to tell me more things to do in life, because now I think you have pretty good advice!

3). How outspoken you are in regard to equality. Keep fighting the good fight.

Anyway, I really appreciate you a whole lot. I hope to get to know you even better from here on out! Seriously. Don't be afraid to contact me at the below information. xo.

Sincerely,
Austin James Robinson

Connor Lee,

If you're reading this, it's because you 'liked' or 'reacted' to a Facebook status I made back in April. I know, it's been awhile and I suck! I expect you to expect me to send you the Cheesecake Factory Menu or something – and honestly I will do that at a later time if you wish, – but this is a letter containing things I appreciate about you.

1). How we met at the HOBY in Maryland and then not even three months later you felt comfortable enough to post a picture of a minion saying a Spy Kids 2 quote on my Facebook. That's true friendship. Cut out all of the bullshit and just go straight for the Minion sharing. I'm so glad we progressed so fast. But seriously, I think we really connected at HOBY – I remember talking to you about shopping at thrift stores and politics or something. Honestly, who can never be sure? Nice time, though.

2). That one time you had hella reading and homework to do, yet you still messaged my drunk ass. *Signs he's the ONE.* **But seriously, I hope you're doing well in school and that you're putting your studies above texting drunk people (or, you know, don't – this is your life and only you can live it).**

Anyway, I really appreciate you a whole lot. I hope to get to know you even better from here on out! Seriously. Don't be afraid to contact me at the below information. xo.

Sincerely,
Austin James Robinson

Cosi Pori,

If you're reading this, it's because you 'liked' or 'reacted' to a Facebook status I made back in April. I know, it's been awhile and I suck! I expect you to expect me to send you the Cheesecake Factory Menu or something – and honestly I will do that at a later time if you wish, – but this is a letter containing things I appreciate about you.

1). The fact that we met on some dating app and are still connected. I think we were both in New Mexico for some reason? But now we're at the opposite ends of the country, which is pretty cool. One day we'll meet and it'll be HUNDRED HUNDRED HUNDRED.

2). The fact that I went on a date with your dance teacher. Lmao, that was so interesting. By the way, we never spoke again after that night. We literally drank wine while watching the US Presidential Election results and then sort of had an unspoken agreement to never speak again. It wasn't even a bad date! Like, it was really cool and we had a lot to talk about. I have no clue what happened, but that's what I love about it all. You know I love being confused!

3). Your eccentricity, but the fact that it's just YOU and you don't even try. You don't give a fucking shit, and that's THE shit. That's really cool and rare to see where I'm from, and I know it is where you're from, too. Keep doing whatever the hell you want, you know.

Anyway, I really appreciate you a whole lot. I hope to get to know you even better from here on out! Seriously. Don't be afraid to contact me at the below information. xo.

Sincerely,
Austin James Robinson

[NAME REDACTED],

If you're reading this, it's because you 'liked' or 'reacted' to a Facebook status I made back in April. I know, it's been awhile and I suck! I expect you to expect me to send you the Cheesecake Factory Menu or something – and honestly I will do that at a later time if you wish, – but this is a letter containing things I appreciate about you.

1). How you [REDACTED] on me and my brand and my service for your [REDACTED] project a couple of years ago. I was so happy when you approached me about wanting to cover some of my volunteer work. Of course, you know I love the attention and all. And I was also really happy when you included a small bit about my brand in the [REDACTED]. Anyway, THANKS FOR THAT. I'm glad we got to remain friends after it!

2). Okay so other than that, we haven't really talked much! So here's a story to end this letter: Have you ever heard about phone sex? Well, one time I was in middle school, and this guy called me and wanted to have phone sex with me for some reason. Weird-o! Anyway, I told him to hold on and then I three-way called my best friend, who ended up actually being the one to engage in phone sex with this guy. But all he kept screaming was, "TERIYAKI TERIYAKI TERIYAKI." Anyway, have a nice day!

Anyway, I really appreciate you a whole lot. I hope to get to know you even better from here on out! Seriously. Don't be afraid to contact me at the below information. xo.

Sincerely,
Austin James Robinson

Crystin Benefield,

If you're reading this, it's because you 'liked' or 'reacted' to a Facebook status I made back in April. I know, it's been awhile and I suck! I expect you to expect me to send you the Cheesecake Factory Menu or something – and honestly I will do that at a later time if you wish, – but this is a letter containing things I appreciate about you.

1). How you stalked me at the Skating Rink back in, like, 2006. Do you remember that? How we met? Because you wouldn't leave me alone and I gave you the 1-800 number that was supposed to tell you "Ha-ha, you've been pranked!" when you call it – but instead my brother decided that it would be really funny to give you my actual number? And then I told my mom and he got in trouble, but at that point you had already sent me, like, 50,000,000 pictures of your unicycle, your various rubber chickens, and your tripp pants? You were so FUCKIN' weird! Anyway, at that moment, I literally became super weird and funny. So, actually, you literally changed my life. Not even exaggerating that. I would be normal af today if that wouldn't have happened. Thanks!

2). That one time you threw your phone at me and then said, "What the heck, man? You just dropped my phone!"

3). The "WHAT? HUH? OH!" joke.

4). We have way too many inside jokes and one-liners, so I'm going to stop there. But yeah, I also like how you have THREE CHILDREN. I cannot wait to see y'all again.

Anyway, I really appreciate you a whole lot. I hope to get to know you even better from here on out! Seriously. Don't be afraid to contact me at the below information. xo.

Sincerely,
Austin James Robinson

Cy Zamanian,

If you're reading this, it's because you 'liked' or 'reacted' to a Facebook status I made back in April. I know, it's been awhile and I suck! I expect you to expect me to send you the Cheesecake Factory Menu or something – and honestly I will do that at a later time if you wish, – but this is a letter containing things I appreciate about you.

1). Your realistic expectations of the world, or how you interact with others and conduct yourself in relation to other human beings. Wow, what a roundabout way to say that I basically think you're very mature in your opinions. Okay, so remember when you messaged me over a year or so ago and you sent me screenshots of an interaction you had with an individual who has more negative SJW tendencies? And you were basically like, "We should all tolerate and accept each other???" and they were like, "Na"? (Lmao, if not, it's in our Messenger conversations.) Anyway, I really admire how you handled that situation and your thought process throughout the entire thing. I think we have similar beliefs and mindsets when it comes to society. Anyway, keep at it because you're one accepting dude.

2). The simple fact that you're in aerospace engineering. I believe we've had an IRL conversation regarding the space industry, but yeah – I freaking love aerospace, and if I had the brain for it, I would totally be doing it right now. I'm so happy you're doing it. Maybe we can speak at lengths about it someday. I can't wait to see where you go in this world in regard to aerospace

Anyway, I really appreciate you a whole lot. I hope to get to know you even better from here on out! Seriously. Don't be afraid to contact me at the below information. xo.

Sincerely,
Austin James Robinson

Dane Stull,

If you're reading this, it's because you 'liked' or 'reacted' to a Facebook status I made back in April. I know, it's been awhile and I suck! I expect you to expect me to send you the Cheesecake Factory Menu or something – and honestly I will do that at a later time if you wish, – but this is a letter containing things I appreciate about you.

1). I don't know where to start, Dane. I honestly don't know where to start. I guess I'll start by thanking you being the kindest and sweetest guy I have ever been in a sort-of relationship with. I know, we can't really define what we were back in November / December. You have been the *only* good guy I have ever dated – and I mean that from the bottom of my heart. I cried after you because I finally felt that I could be loved and not be with men who just want to bring me down. I really should have stayed with you, but this is not a letter regarding regrets – it is a letter about how you changed me.

2). You deserve every single thing in the world. You are so happy right now and you are in a grand relationship. And I love that. That makes me happy. You don't deserve sadness – you don't deserve heartache. Who you are – everything that makes you, you – is everything beautiful in the world, and I just can't believe I got to experience you.

3). Okay, so this has more-or-less just turned into a sappy letter opposed to me listing off things I appreciate about you, and I apologize for that. But I wish there was a way I could honestly show you how I feel about you entering my life. It may not seem like much to you, but you have shown me so much beauty and how a relationship should be. In less than a month. Can you believe that? Did it feel like less than a month to you? It felt like forever to me. But forever

always ends. I'm so happy it happened.

Anyway, I really appreciate you a whole lot. I hope to get to know you even better from here on out! Seriously. Don't be afraid to contact me at the below information. xo.

Sincerely,
Austin James Robinson

Dang Ton,

If you're reading this, it's because you 'liked' or 'reacted' to a Facebook status I made back in April. I know, it's been awhile and I suck! I expect you to expect me to send you the Cheesecake Factory Menu or something – and honestly I will do that at a later time if you wish, – but this is a letter containing things I appreciate about you.

1). Your name, of course. But we all know that. We all love it. It's iconic. Amen.

2). Your love for your stuffed Alpaca, and how it's basically taken over your social media. Thank God for that. Also, I'm pretty sure you're the one running the Auston Jomes Robonson page. I think you told me that once, but honestly who can never be sure?

3). Your passion for service + your weirdness. Not a lot of people who love volunteering and helping the world are weird – I mean, a lot of people in APO are weird, but idk, they're not DANG weird. Which is a good thing. But also, you super love volunteering and helping change the world through APO – and that's also a thing that not a lot of people can say. You truly care.

4). A fourth thing!

Anyway, I really appreciate you a whole lot. I hope to get to know you even better from here on out! Seriously. Don't be afraid to contact me at the below information. xo.

Sincerely,
Austin James Robinson

Daniel Smarda,

If you're reading this, it's because you 'liked' or 'reacted' to a Facebook status I made back in April. I know, it's been awhile and I suck! I expect you to expect me to send you the Cheesecake Factory Menu or something – and honestly I will do that at a later time if you wish, – but this is a letter containing things I appreciate about you.

1). The fact that you were the only other person in Texas Blazers who was also in Alpha Phi Omega. Oh shoot, it looks like I forgot about Gregory Ross. Well, he was never *really* in APO anyway. Are you even still in APO? Who cares – as long as you are in Texas Blazers. This point has gone on too long.

2). That time we sat together on the SAC rooftop just talking about life and choices and everything in between. That was a really nice time. You had so many choices to make, and you were really worried about all of them. Now look where you're at. I can imagine you are much happier and do not regret a thing. I'm happy for you and the choices you ended up making.

3). This one is small, but remember when I was driving and then saw you, so I stopped and you were all: "I'm literally going to the airport right now to leave for Study Abroad." I just love that I was able to say bye to you literally right before you left. Serendipitous.

Anyway, I really appreciate you a whole lot. I hope to get to know you even better from here on out! Seriously. Don't be afraid to contact me at the below information. xo.

Sincerely,
Austin James Robinson

Daniel Stroik,

If you're reading this, it's because you 'liked' or 'reacted' to a Facebook status I made back in April. I know, it's been awhile and I suck! I expect you to expect me to send you the Cheesecake Factory Menu or something – and honestly I will do that at a later time if you wish, – but this is a letter containing things I appreciate about you.

1). Our weird-ass "group" during that whole summer business thing we did (before I dropped out). I can't believe we all sat in front of every class we were in and created general havoc among the class. Literally, who were we? Why was that a thing that we all collectively decided to do. Sorry I left!

2). Your loyalty to my BRAND. I remember when you were the first person to buy my shirt via PayPal on my website. I thought that was pretty fun – usually everyone just buys it by messaging me and then venmoing me the money. Anyway, and then you were apart of my "focus group" for my energy drink (AJR H2O), which I ended up giving you. Hopefully it was good. Fun times.

3). How could I forget: HONORABLE MENTION. Honestly, I'm still not entirely sure how you're connected to that band whatsoever. What I do remember is you just continuously telling everyone to listen to them on Spotify throughout our summer business program. God bless.

Anyway, I really appreciate you a whole lot. I hope to get to know you even better from here on out! Seriously. Don't be afraid to contact me at the below information. xo.

Sincerely,
Austin James Robinson

Danny Murray,

If you're reading this, it's because you 'liked' or 'reacted' to a Facebook status I made back in April. I know, it's been awhile and I suck! I expect you to expect me to send you the Cheesecake Factory Menu or something – and honestly I will do that at a later time if you wish, – but this is a letter containing things I appreciate about you.

1). How in love with the 80s you are. To the point where I'm pretty sure you actually think we're living in the 80s right at this second. Is that why you won't watch Black Mirror with me? Because technically it wasn't around in the 80s? That's literally the only reason I can think of. Wow, that's dedication right there.

2). How we were the only two Texas Blazers who were in the College of Education. I don't care if you come back with "oh but wait wasn't so-and-so also in Education??" – no, we were the only two members in the College of Education. However, we were very different in our concentrations. Although, I loved having someone I could go up to and be all, "So I have a question… how do I work out??? Like, how?"

3). How you keep posting pictures of you on top of mountains and I have to keep telling you to be careful. There's really nothing else to say here – just be careful when you're on top of rocks, Danny!

Anyway, I really appreciate you a whole lot. I hope to get to know you even better from here on out! Seriously. Don't be afraid to contact me at the below information. xo.

Sincerely,
Austin James Robinson

[NAME REDACTED],

If you're reading this, it's because you 'liked' or 'reacted' to a Facebook status I made back in April. I know, it's been awhile and I suck! I expect you to expect me to send you the Cheesecake Factory Menu or something – and honestly I will do that at a later time if you wish, – but this is a letter containing things I appreciate about you.

1). The fact that our friendship is really weird and dumb. We just send jokes and memes and naughty emoji chain texts to each other. And we'll occasionally (like, once) eat at [REDACTED]. But regardless, you're ALWAYS there to be dumb with me.

2). Your [REDACTED] skills. You're probably the best [REDACTED] the [REDACTED] ever had. But you know that. And I hope you go on to [REDACTED] anything and EVERYTHING. Do [REDACTED] for [REDACTED] or something! I heard that's a thing!

3). How you were the only person on all of my social media that even cared about my mysterious photo posts when I was in [REDACTED]. Do you remember that? It seems like a distant memory, even to me. But you kept guessing where I was every day. Blessed.

Anyway, I really appreciate you a whole lot. I hope to get to know you even better from here on out! Seriously. Don't be afraid to contact me at the below information. xo.

Sincerely,
Austin James Robinson

Dawn Stewart,

If you're reading this, it's because you 'liked' or 'reacted' to a Facebook status I made back in April. I know, it's been awhile and I suck! I expect you to expect me to send you the Cheesecake Factory Menu or something – and honestly I will do that at a later time if you wish, – but this is a letter containing things I appreciate about you.

1). The fact that we met in Circle K International, like, four years ago or something like that, and we're still friends! I love when that happens – especially when the person isn't from the same area or school as me. I remember you always being one of the sweetest people I've ever met in CKI and in general. Keep being absolutely amazing!

2). The fact that you're a Music Therapist now and are thinking about writing a book to help other people! I absolutely adore that you are looking to serve people even outside of your extracurricular activities. You are making a life of helping other people – you are truly going to change the world one day.

3). How you work with individuals with intellectual and/or developmental disabilities. Again, another example of how extremely selfless you are. Thank you for all that you do!!!

Anyway, I really appreciate you a whole lot. I hope to get to know you even better from here on out! Seriously. Don't be afraid to contact me at the below information. xo.

Sincerely,
Austin James Robinson

Debbie Nehikhuere,

If you're reading this, it's because you 'liked' or 'reacted' to a Facebook status I made back in April. I know, it's been awhile and I suck! I expect you to expect me to send you the Cheesecake Factory Menu or something – and honestly I will do that at a later time if you wish, – but this is a letter containing things I appreciate about you.

1). Meeting you on the set of The 40. I'm so happy that you ended up coming on and helping us make The 40 a reality. You meant so much to me and everyone who helped start the show, and I miss being able to see you every week and think of show ideas with you! I hope you stay with The 40 well after all of us have graduated and left – maybe you can keep it alive!

2). I guess other than The 40, we haven't really talked or gotten to know each other. So, here's a story to end this letter and take away from the fact that I don't know what else to write: one time in high school, my boyfriend cheated on me, so I got him back by spreading a rumor that he leaked poop because he had a gastrointestinal disease. Anyway, bye!

Anyway, I really appreciate you a whole lot. I hope to get to know you even better from here on out! Seriously. Don't be afraid to contact me at the below information. xo.

Sincerely,
Austin James Robinson

Delisa Shannon,

If you're reading this, it's because you 'liked' or 'reacted' to a Facebook status I made back in April. I know, it's been awhile and I suck! I expect you to expect me to send you the Cheesecake Factory Menu or something – and honestly I will do that at a later time if you wish, – but this is a letter containing things I appreciate about you.

1). Where do I even freaking start??? I guess where it all began. YOU RAN SUCH A GOOD STUDENT GOVERNMENT EXECUTIVE ALLIANCE CAMPAIGN. I mean, I pretty much told y'all constantly: I almost voted for y'all instead of myself. LOL. Honestly it should have been between y'all and us (don't tell anyone I said that). I wish we could do it all over again.

2). THE FACT THAT YOU INVITED ME TO HELP START THE 40. I cry every day because I had to leave due to the fact that I graduated early. I wish I could still help out. It provided me with some of the best experiences during my college career. And I always keep up with it, and I love how much it has grown. I know you'll be leaving soon, so honestly I expect the entirety of the campus to COLLAPSE because you'll be gone.

3). Your social media. Sorry, but no one else can compete. You have the most hilarious and most important posts all across social media. I hope I'm in your life FOREVER.

Anyway, I really appreciate you a whole lot. I hope to get to know you even better from here on out! Seriously. Don't be afraid to contact me at the below information. xo.

Sincerely,
Austin James Robinson

PROJECT LETTERS

Derick Kirksey,

If you're reading this, it's because you 'liked' or 'reacted' to a Facebook status I made back in April. I know, it's been awhile and I suck! I expect you to expect me to send you the Cheesecake Factory Menu or something – and honestly I will do that at a later time if you wish, – but this is a letter containing things I appreciate about you.

1). How willing you were to let me stay at your place for, like, a week even though you had no clue who I was. I mean, I know Stephen's really the one I went through to ask and whatnot, but still: it's your place too, and I'm really happy there are people like you and Stephen out there who are willing to help people out when they need a place to stay.

2). Your apparent "zero-bullshit" policy and how well you execute it. Remember when we were walking around DC and getting coffee at Starbucks and yadda yadda, and then Stephen needed something from home and wanted you to bring it to him? LOL, you were hilarious with your actions, but it showed that you sort of don't take shit from anyone and you live your own life. Idk, I hope Stephen doesn't read this part because I couldn't word it properly and now it just seems like we ignored a friend in a time of need. Omg.

3). Your extensive knowledge on Columbine. Okay, maybe this isn't the best point, but I remember becoming obsessed with that book Stephen has and you already knowing a lot of details. I mean, I know you lived to hear about it on the news and all (whereas I was a baby), but still.

Anyway, I really appreciate you a whole lot. I hope to get to know you even better from here on out! Seriously. Don't be afraid to contact me at the below information. xo.

Sincerely,
Austin James Robinson

Destiny Salazar,

If you're reading this, it's because you 'liked' or 'reacted' to a Facebook status I made back in April. I know, it's been awhile and I suck! I expect you to expect me to send you the Cheesecake Factory Menu or something – and honestly I will do that at a later time if you wish, – but this is a letter containing things I appreciate about you.

1). Your glow-up, but consistent personality. It's no secret that you should totally be a model now (why aren't you doing that?), but you've also kept the same beautiful and inspiring personality throughout our entire friendship (which has existed for, what, 50 years probably?). That's really cool. Never change.

2). Your journey to find yourself and how you don't really allow external factors to influence it. Look, we're all trying to find ourselves in this time in life – duh! But you've recently been trying different things and going with the flow and doing what you want to do, and that's really cool. You don't allow other people to influence your decisions or direction in life. It might suck right now because, like, what's happening??? But it all works out, and I know you know that.

3). Okay, so this is more of a story. Remember those Left Behind books you always had in your house? And how I would always attempt to read them and never got far at all and this was a struggle I had, like, my entire upbringing? Did you ever read those? I can't remember. Also, what the hell were those even about? I'm still so confused, in general. I should read them now.

Anyway, I really appreciate you a whole lot. I hope to get to know you even better from here on out! Seriously. Don't be afraid to contact me at the below information. xo.

Sincerely,
Austin James Robinson

Divine Ntomchukwu,

If you're reading this, it's because you 'liked' or 'reacted' to a Facebook status I made back in April. I know, it's been awhile and I suck! I expect you to expect me to send you the Cheesecake Factory Menu or something – and honestly I will do that at a later time if you wish, – but this is a letter containing things I appreciate about you.

1). How dedicated you are to Student Government. From campaigning to *almost* being able to run for office (sorry – not meaning to bring it up – I think you still should have been able to), you have shown that you completely adore and believe in the governing organization of UT, and UT as a whole, really. Keep it up.

2). The fact that you're a University Co-op model. Excuse me, what? When I saw your face plastered on, like, half of the co-op building, I almost DIED. How the HELL did you even do that? And why am I suddenly jealous????? But honestly, you should be a literal model. Do that.

3). The fact that your literal first ever message to me on any texting platform was about how you heard the song "NO" by Meghan Trainor and then immediately thought of me. That is the sweetest thing anyone has ever said to me.

Anyway, I really appreciate you a whole lot. I hope to get to know you even better from here on out! Seriously. Don't be afraid to contact me at the below information. xo.

Sincerely,
Austin James Robinson

DJ Roberts,

If you're reading this, it's because you 'liked' or 'reacted' to a Facebook status I made back in April. I know, it's been awhile and I suck! I expect you to expect me to send you the Cheesecake Factory Menu or something – and honestly I will do that at a later time if you wish, – but this is a letter containing things I appreciate about you.

1). How I feel like you were the first funny person I ever met at the university. I remember following you on Twitter not even knowing who you were (I also feel like you definitely had a following at that point – I remember thinking you were, like, famous or some shit). And your tweets were just hilarious. Then I got to know you and you kind of ruined that perception. Kidding – you're still O.K. But now I get to be good friends with a funny Twitter guy! Yay!

2). The fact that you're the only other person in my life who is obsessed with Little Free Libraries. I literally became obsessed with the concept once I walked past one in LA, and I completely forgot about them (such a great obsession, huh) until you brought them up at a Texas Blazers meeting. I'm so sorry I dropped the ball and didn't become apart of that committee (I think this was around the time I was trying to take over Student Government or something – IDK). Anyway, CALL ME SOME TIME SO WE CAN DISCUSS LITTLE FREE LIBRARIES.

Anyway, I really appreciate you a whole lot. I hope to get to know you even better from here on out! Seriously. Don't be afraid to contact me at the below information. xo.

Sincerely,
Austin James Robinson

Doug Snyder,

If you're reading this, it's because you 'liked' or 'reacted' to a Facebook status I made back in April. I know, it's been awhile and I suck! I expect you to expect me to send you the Cheesecake Factory Menu or something – and honestly I will do that at a later time if you wish, – but this is a letter containing things I appreciate about you.

1). Your sense of humor AND fashion. You are funny af, and you know that. And you also dress great. What?! That's a PACKAGE right there. But seriously, you know how to take everyday, casual conversations about society and make them humorous. All the while wearing dope clothes that totally distract from the jokes. Iconic.

2). That time we matched on a popular dating app, but you're straight and I'm gay. Yeah, I still don't know what happened, but it WAS a conversation starter and basically the only reason we truly started chatting. So, I guess thank God for that. They may not know how to match sexually compatible people, but they do know how to make the most out of friendship <3

3). Your dedication to University Democrats and, like, voting and stuff. Keep registering people to vote and spreading word about civic duties and whatnot!

Anyway, I really appreciate you a whole lot. I hope to get to know you even better from here on out! Seriously. Don't be afraid to contact me at the below information. xo.

Sincerely,
Austin James Robinson

DVNOTS,

If you're reading this, it's because you 'liked' or 'reacted' to a Facebook status I made back in April. I know, it's been awhile and I suck! I expect you to expect me to send you the Cheesecake Factory Menu or something – and honestly I will do that at a later time if you wish, – but this is a letter containing things I appreciate about you.

1). Okay before we get started, I'm using your DJ / Producer / Artist name because that's mainly how I know you by and also YOU HAVEN'T PICKED OUT A NAME YET!! I'm super excited to hear it, by the way. Keep me updated x. Oh awk, I guess this wasn't too much of a point. Oh well.

2). How absolutely amazing you are at music. I don't even know how to use a computer, and yet you're over there making beats that I literally have downloaded on my ITUNES. And you're what? 12 years old? (I know you're older – I just wanted to hyperbolize how young you are compared to me, and now the joke is ruined because I decided to explain it. But I didn't want you to get offended in the case you thought that I thought that you are actually 12. What is anything I'm saying right now?)

3). How I literally feel like I was a creepy stan and now I'm writing you a letter. Literally, I Googled you for a good 30 minutes once and found you playing Maps by the Yeah Yeah Yeahs on stage via YouTube, among other things. I was weird af because I just thought you made the coolest music ever. I thought it was hella cool when we started following each other on Twitter a couple years ago. Then you became good friends with [REDACTED] and I knew that was my IN. Now we're good friends but I promise I'm SIGNIFICANTLY less creepy. Thank God. Amen.

Anyway, I really appreciate you a whole lot. I hope to get to know you even better from here on out! Seriously. Don't be afraid to contact me at the below information. xo.

Sincerely,
Austin James Robinson

UPDATE: Her name is Lilah <3

Eamon Dowd,

If you're reading this, it's because you 'liked' or 'reacted' to a Facebook status I made back in April. I know, it's been awhile and I suck! I expect you to expect me to send you the Cheesecake Factory Menu or something – and honestly I will do that at a later time if you wish, – but this is a letter containing things I appreciate about you.

1). The amount of majors you have. Just do you. I have no clue what the hell you're going to be when you grow up (we're all little babies right now, and possibly forever), but I'm really excited to know you when you become the world's best renaissance man.

2). The fact that you look like Danny L Harle, the world's best DJ right now. Sometimes I'll start crying when I'm around you because I think you're actually him and then I have to remind myself that I'm actually crying because you're Eamon, and that's just as special.

3). Your future book. We all know you're going to write a book someday. And, idk, I think you have the best chance of writing a bestseller out of everyone I know. I don't even know why! I'm pretty sure none of your majors have to do with writing or anything related to book making. But I guess that's the mystery that none of us ever find out.

Anyway, I really appreciate you a whole lot. I hope to get to know you even better from here on out! Seriously. Don't be afraid to contact me at the below information. xo.

Sincerely,
Austin James Robinson

Ed Kim,

If you're reading this, it's because you 'liked' or 'reacted' to a Facebook status I made back in April. I know, it's been awhile and I suck! I expect you to expect me to send you the Cheesecake Factory Menu or something – and honestly I will do that at a later time if you wish, – but this is a letter containing things I appreciate about you.

1). Of course I have to start this off by saying how dope of a time we had together at Stanford University during the JSA Summer School. You and [REDACTED] were literally the funniest people there (besides Kate Bell, but who could beat Kate Bell?). I'm so glad I ended up going to JSA if only because of you and [REDACTED].

2). Remember when I came to LA and ended up hanging out with you and [REDACTED] in the Palisades and on the beach? I would stop bringing [REDACTED] up, but you know that's impossible. I basically snuck into your school past the security guards and then went into the library to wait for y'all to be done with school for the day. Wild times.

3). Kiwins. And of course I have to bring up Kiwins. I still have no freaking clue what the hell Kiwins is. I just remember you being so into it and finding out that it's related to Key Club, but never having heard of it before in my life (even though I was obsessed with everything Kiwanis related).

Anyway, I really appreciate you a whole lot. I hope to get to know you even better from here on out! Seriously. Don't be afraid to contact me at the below information. xo.

Sincerely,
Austin James Robinson

Eddie Babbe,

If you're reading this, it's because you 'liked' or 'reacted' to a Facebook status I made back in April. I know, it's been awhile and I suck! I expect you to expect me to send you the Cheesecake Factory Menu or something – and honestly I will do that at a later time if you wish, – but this is a letter containing things I appreciate about you.

1). Your sense of humor. Your sense of humor is something that I couldn't pinpoint for the longest time. I guess we never really hung out, and honestly I was probably scared of you. But I remember the day I realized we have at least somewhat similar senses of humor. It was before a meeting in the UTC and we discussed how much we love pranking other people. It's one of my life-long dreams to be able to pull off pranks with you. Sort of PUNK'd-like, but way better and not as mid-2000s. Like, maybe more Nathan For You styled punking? Have you ever seen that show? What if we had our own show? Anyway…

2). Your politics, or rather, the different point of view you bring to Texas Blazers, UT, and Austin. I don't think it's a secret that everyone knows you're pretty conservative. At least, I hear that about you a lot. I guess I've never totally asked. And I don't mean I've heard that as in people are saying, "woah did you hear Eddie is a Republican????" – I guess politics is just brought up a lot at an institution with intellectuals. Anyway, I really appreciate it because there are way too many liberal people everywhere – Texas Blazers, UT, and Austin. It is incredibly refreshing to not be around the same type of people constantly. (Plus I think Blazers – especially nowadays – seriously needs more conservative-type people. Is that shitty of me to say? Oh well.)

Anyway, I really appreciate you a whole lot. I hope to get to know you even better from here on out! Seriously. Don't be afraid to contact me at the below information. xo.

Sincerely,
Austin James Robinson

[NAME REDACTED],

If you're reading this, it's because you 'liked' or 'reacted' to a Facebook status I made back in April. I know, it's been awhile and I suck! I expect you to expect me to send you the Cheesecake Factory Menu or something – and honestly I will do that at a later time if you wish, – but this is a letter containing things I appreciate about you.

1). THAT TIME YOU CAME TO CLASS IN [REDACTED]. What the hell – that was literally the greatest moments of all of our lives, and if any of those students try to argue that, I will personally set up a debate tournament entirely around how that totally was the best moment of our lives. The professor was LIVING that day. I can't believe I never saw you [REDACTED] in a typical setting, but I saw you [REDACTED] in CLASS. I'm still laughing.

2). OUR [REDACTED] ADVENTURES TOGETHER. Remember when we both arrived in [REDACTED] at the same exact time and we were like, "How does money even work??" and everyone around us was probably like, "Look at these idiots?" Well, I'm just glad I didn't have to be clueless alone. And then we had a kickass time in [REDACTED] in general. I wish we could do it all over again.

3). How caring and amazing you are to other people. I'm pretty sure I've never seen you be mean to anyone else or be mad. You truly care about other people and have one of the nicest personalities I've ever seen. Keep that up, because a lot of people aren't nice. I personally think it's the single best trait someone could have.

Anyway, I really appreciate you a whole lot. I hope to get to know you even better from here on out! Seriously. Don't be afraid to contact me at the below information. xo.

Sincerely,
Austin James Robinson

Erik Margetis,

If you're reading this, it's because you 'liked' or 'reacted' to a Facebook status I made back in April. I know, it's been awhile and I suck! I expect you to expect me to send you the Cheesecake Factory Menu or something – and honestly I will do that at a later time if you wish, – but this is a letter containing things I appreciate about you.

1). The fact that we are both Greek and, thus, are brothers forever. Okay, maybe that's not a real thing, but I do find it cool that you and Thanos are basically the only two Greek guys I've ever been friends with. I'm just from a small place where no one is Greek. So, I guess thanks for being Greek??

2). How you're a constant supporter of my brand. You bought the AJR shirt while you were doing Study Abroad – you basically had it on hold for a whole semester. And I love when you wear it to Texas Blazers events and subject everyone to it and they're just sort of like, "Shit – we thought that was over." Thanks for reminding everyone that my shirt is COOL. Likewise, when I was running for Student Body Vice President, you were more than willing to support me and market my campaign – even though I'm pretty sure that's when you were doing Study Abroad. I'm sure all of the friends you were making over there thought you were weird.

3). KPs! Of course I'm going to bring up your new business venture. What the hell, dude, that's SO cool! I cannot wait to own literally several pairs (and I'm not kidding about that). I hope they become way more famous than any other casual-wear shoe, because God knows they look better than the rest of them.

4). How everyone constantly digs up your old Facebook content. I hope that never ends.

Anyway, I really appreciate you a whole lot. I hope to get to know you even better from here on out! Seriously. Don't be afraid to contact me at the below information. xo.

Sincerely,
Austin James Robinson

Erika Ong,

If you're reading this, it's because you 'liked' or 'reacted' to a Facebook status I made back in April. I know, it's been awhile and I suck! I expect you to expect me to send you the Cheesecake Factory Menu or something – and honestly I will do that at a later time if you wish, – but this is a letter containing things I appreciate about you.

1). YOUR, LIKE, UNDYING DEDICATION TO TEXAS THON. Dang, girl, you are so freaking good at what you do for Texas THON. I've been to two Texas THONs, but you make me feel like I'm doing NOTHING #ForTheKids. But for real, like, I wish I could do more and you inspire me to go out and do just that. I'm so happy you're now the president of Texas THON. You are going to raise so much money, and go down in history.

2). However, I think I know you because of Senate of College Councils (college is one big blur to me, honestly). Also, if I'm not mistaken, you have some ties to Camp Texas? I honestly can't keep up. I feel like I know you from so many different things because you are just so incredibly involved. And I love that! You are for sure going to change the world someday.

Anyway, I really appreciate you a whole lot. I hope to get to know you even better from here on out! Seriously. Don't be afraid to contact me at the below information. xo.

Sincerely,
Austin James Robinson

Ehtan Nouri,

If you're reading this, it's because you 'liked' or 'reacted' to a Facebook status I made back in April. I know, it's been awhile and I suck! I expect you to expect me to send you the Cheesecake Factory Menu or something – and honestly I will do that at a later time if you wish, – but this is a letter containing things I appreciate about you.

1). I love the fact that we volunteered for, like, seven days together at South By Southwest. That was such a surreal time for me. I had never been to SXSW and I have not been back since (and literally I didn't really go to anything during my time volunteering there). I just remember taking a picture of [REDACTED] peeing at the urinal, which was apparently very illegal. Oops. Anyway, this is supposed to be about you – NOT ME. You were basically the coolest person who volunteered with me. Unlike that one lady who tried to be our manager once or something (do you remember that? Were you there for that?). Wild stuff.

2). Anyway, then we saw each other a couple of times on campus, and that was really cool. I love how easy-going you are, and how willing you are to make friends with people.

Anyway, I really appreciate you a whole lot. I hope to get to know you even better from here on out! Seriously. Don't be afraid to contact me at the below information. xo.

Sincerely,
Austin James Robinson

[NAME REDACTED],

If you're reading this, it's because you 'liked' or 'reacted' to a Facebook status I made back in April. I know, it's been awhile and I suck! I expect you to expect me to send you the Cheesecake Factory Menu or something – and honestly I will do that at a later time if you wish, – but this is a letter containing things I appreciate about you.

1). That time we went on a date to that amazing Italian place and then didn't speak to each other for a long time after that. Haha, sounds dumb, but I always appreciate those times when you reconnect with someone that you never expected to. And I love the fact that you apologized to me for essentially ghosting me (in a sense – I know it wasn't full on ghosting considering you had no obligation to me at all), because a lot of people don't end up apologizing for their actions. Anyway, I'm just glad we're still friends after all of that.

2). In a similar situation, remember when we hooked up and I told you that you have a nice body, and you said, "No one's ever old me that before." That was a nice night, even though it was literally just a one-time hookup.

3). How dedicated you are to [REDACTED]. I know you're primarily dedicated to your [REDACTED], but I love that you applied to [REDACTED]. Definitely keep applying! I think you'd be great in [REDACTED].

Anyway, I really appreciate you a whole lot. I hope to get to know you even better from here on out! Seriously. Don't be afraid to contact me at the below information. xo.

Sincerely,
Austin James Robinson

friopalope,

If you're reading this, it's because you 'liked' or 'reacted' to a Facebook status I made back in April. I know, it's been awhile and I suck! I expect you to expect me to send you the Cheesecake Factory Menu or something – and honestly I will do that at a later time if you wish, – but this is a letter containing things I appreciate about you.

1). The fact that we have actually read the Cheesecake Factory Menu together. Now THAT is an experience – and it also means that I don't really need to send it to you. I miss White John ☹ I wish all three of us would have hung out more while I was in Austin. But now he's leaving (if I'm not mistaken) and you're graduating soon (again, if I'm not mistaken) and we may be all over the place. Oh well! Let's keep in touch forever!

2). The fact that I know you outside of the PC Music forums. All of us have lives outside of the PC Music forums, but you're one of the few that I have gotten to know to the point where I don't think "PC Music Forums" when I think about you. I think about how you're incredibly gifted with an eye for beautiful aesthetics and have a kick-ass Instagram that showcases them; and how you're in law school at the same school I went to; and your amazing outfits. Etc. Also almost everyone in that forum is a DJ and that's basically their entire outside life – so I sort of appreciate how you do so much outside of music.

Anyway, I really appreciate you a whole lot. I hope to get to know you even better from here on out! Seriously. Don't be afraid to contact me at the below information. xo.

Sincerely,
Austin James Robinson

Garrett Maples,

If you're reading this, it's because you 'liked' or 'reacted' to a Facebook status I made back in April. I know, it's been awhile and I suck! I expect you to expect me to send you the Cheesecake Factory Menu or something – and honestly I will do that at a later time if you wish, – but this is a letter containing things I appreciate about you.

1). Your mom. Okay, I know this point isn't technically about you, but why is your mom so cool???? She literally made Texas Blazers what it is today, honestly. She's the only reason I got in, probably. She's everything.

2). The fact that you take your shirt off every single time you get drunk. And that's what I've always loved about you. We need more people like you who will get completely naked when they simply smell alcohol. The world would be a better place. (Although, full disclosure, I've never gotten drunk with you and, thus, have actually never been around you when you took your shirt off.)

3). Your bubbly and inspiring personality. Not only are you one of the nicest guys I've ever met, but you also give yourself to everyone in your life – whether it be friends or strangers. I'm literally in love with you. Never stop.

Anyway, I really appreciate you a whole lot. I hope to get to know you even better from here on out! Seriously. Don't be afraid to contact me at the below information. xo.

Sincerely,
Austin James Robinson

Garrett Owen,

If you're reading this, it's because you 'liked' or 'reacted' to a Facebook status I made back in April. I know, it's been awhile and I suck! I expect you to expect me to send you the Cheesecake Factory Menu or something – and honestly I will do that at a later time if you wish, – but this is a letter containing things I appreciate about you.

1). The fact that you went to the University of Colorado Boulder. Idk, I went there once and also have a couple of credit hours from that university. So, that's pretty cool! I think you're literally the only friend I have from that university, so yay! You're the representative!

2). How you're my 'son' on Facebook. I'm not sure if you remember that, but you're most definitely my son on my Facebook family on my about page. Anyway, surprise! Okay wait, I just checked and apparently it's "pending." So… you're technically not my son – but, like, the jury is still out. I'll take it.

3). EGGMA. Remember Eggma? Remember wearing my shirt? Remember the memories? Yeah, those are really the only ones you need to remember. I'm glad I could provide you with those – you're welcome.

4). A fourth thing! Let's make a fourth thing to appreciate together in the future!

Anyway, I really appreciate you a whole lot. I hope to get to know you even better from here on out! Seriously. Don't be afraid to contact me at the below information. xo.

Sincerely,
Austin James Robinson

PROJECT LETTERS

Gregory Boyd,

If you're reading this, it's because you 'liked' or 'reacted' to a Facebook status I made back in April. I know, it's been awhile and I suck! I expect you to expect me to send you the Cheesecake Factory Menu or something – and honestly I will do that at a later time if you wish, – but this is a letter containing things I appreciate about you.

1). The fact that we met each other because of Hugh O'Brian Youth Leadership. Just imagine if we both wouldn't have gone through HOBY and continued to volunteer for it – we wouldn't have met. I love thinking about stuff like that. I'm glad we met though!

2). That time you messaged me telling me that the song "Hey QT" by QT was very addicting. I thought that was so funny because it annoys the hell out of so many other people. Even though I think you said it wasn't very intelligent, I still loved that you at least liked the sound of it!

3). I don't really have a third point, but here's a story: one time I stole a bone from the catacombs in Paris, France. I just stuck it in my shoe and the guard didn't even notice or find out! But then I realized that when I came back to the US, they'd check my shoes. And I didn't want to mail a bone to my home. So, I buried it in front of my AirBNB. Anyway, that was probably a really shitty thing of me to do.

Anyway, I really appreciate you a whole lot. I hope to get to know you even better from here on out! Seriously. Don't be afraid to contact me at the below information. xo.

Sincerely,
Austin James Robinson

Gregory Ross,

If you're reading this, it's because you 'liked' or 'reacted' to a Facebook status I made back in April. I know, it's been awhile and I suck! I expect you to expect me to send you the Cheesecake Factory Menu or something – and honestly I will do that at a later time if you wish, – but this is a letter containing things I appreciate about you.

1). That time we walked the campus of St. Edwards (I think) late at night and then proceeded to go to a lit apartment party where I handed out my energy drinks and you sort of just stood there. Honestly, now that I'm thinking about that: did it even happen? I legitimately cannot remember if the second half of the story is even true. Should I even put this in here if I don't know?

2). How close you and David Engleman are and it makes me smile.

3). How rude you are to me. Remember when we were supposed to see each other in Washington D.C. for MY birthday? Yeah, guess who dropped the ball on that. Oh, and remember when you stalked my résumé online and then tried to point out flaws that you felt were in it, when in reality there were actually no flaws because I'm, what? FLAWLESS. Yeah idk – stop trying to come for me is what the lesson here is, I guess. But you know this is what I've always loved about you.

4). How I know you back from the Key Club days, but didn't actually know you back then. But we can always pretend. Also, we're both in love with Rebecca Riley, so there's something in common!

5). How your voicemail is still how it was when you were 12.

Anyway, I really appreciate you a whole lot. I hope to get to know you even better from here on out! Seriously. Don't be afraid to contact me at the below information. xo.

Sincerely,
Austin James Robinson

PROJECT LETTERS

[NAME REDACTED],

If you're reading this, it's because you 'liked' or 'reacted' to a Facebook status I made back in April. I know, it's been awhile and I suck! I expect you to expect me to send you the Cheesecake Factory Menu or something – and honestly I will do that at a later time if you wish, – but this is a letter containing things I appreciate about you.

1). I'm going to be honest: I have no clue who you are. I'm not sure how we became friends on Facebook or what you know about me, but regardless, I am thankful you liked my status and are willing to receive a letter from an absolute stranger. However, because I don't know much about you, I can't really write an entire page worth of stuff regarding what I appreciate about you. And saying, "You're hot!" will only cover so many words. So, I'll tell you a story instead:

2). Okay, so you know Gwen Stefani? I love her so much. In fact, I love her to the point where her first two albums (and really only because I'm not counting the new one) were what I listened to in order to go to sleep literally both in 5th and 6th grades. I brought her inaugural solo album entitled "LOVE. ANGEL. MUSIC. BABY. (LAMB)" to school with me in 5th grade because I just loved it so much and wanted to tell everyone about it. Well, I didn't get too far in my mission because during breakfast, the school police officer saw me holding the album and took it away from me. Later on, the principal called me in and told me that the album displayed a "half-naked woman" and was "inappropriate for school." Being a gay-ass kid, I was like, "What's a woman??" Anyway, I wasn't allowed to bring her next CD to school either because she was also basically naked on that cover. ☹

Anyway, I really appreciate you a whole lot. I hope to get to know you even better from here on out! Seriously. Don't be afraid to contact me at the below information. xo.

Sincerely,
Austin James Robinson

Hannah Conrad,

If you're reading this, it's because you 'liked' or 'reacted' to a Facebook status I made back in April. I know, it's been awhile and I suck! I expect you to expect me to send you the Cheesecake Factory Menu or something – and honestly I will do that at a later time if you wish, – but this is a letter containing things I appreciate about you.

1). The fact that we do Hugh O'Brian Youth Leadership together! That's always a fun bond that not many people have with each other. So I especially love my HOBY mates. But other than that, we don't really talk! So I don't have much to go off of to warrant a whole letter about what I appreciate about you ☹ But instead of bullshitting content, I'll share a story about Tide Pods:

2). Okay, so during HOBY's 2015 seminar, there was this ambassador who I was talking with. He totally casually dropped that his sister DESIGNED THE TIDE POD. You know, the detergent balls that you just throw inside your washing machine so you don't have to mess with all of that liquid?? Yeah, his sister did that. Anyway, I've ONLY bought and used Tide Pods since then. And I suggest you do the same! Thanks!

Anyway, I really appreciate you a whole lot. I hope to get to know you even better from here on out! Seriously. Don't be afraid to contact me at the below information. xo.

Sincerely,
Austin James Robinson

Hannah Schake,

If you're reading this, it's because you 'liked' or 'reacted' to a Facebook status I made back in April. I know, it's been awhile and I suck! I expect you to expect me to send you the Cheesecake Factory Menu or something – and honestly I will do that at a later time if you wish, – but this is a letter containing things I appreciate about you.

1). The fact that we were in TSSA together. I'm pretty sure that organization (or whatever it was) is totally dead now. So, there's only so many people who have this experience and these memories together! So, I'm super happy that we have that in common. However, it's no secret that we don't really know each other because we haven't really talked since our TSSA days. So, I want to end this by telling you a story:

2). So, this one summer in my hometown (which is a very small town in the middle of nowhere, Texas), this girl was grounded for the whole summer. She decided, "If I'm going to be grounded and do nothing all summer, I might as well DRESS UP AS A CLOWN AND STAND ON THE STREET CORNER OF A BUSY STREET FOR EIGHT HOURS EACH DAY." Literally, that was her thought process. This tore our entire town up. People were PISSED. People were LOSING THEIR SHIT. They didn't know what to do. It was as if they had never seen a clown before, or that this was the worst possible thing that could ever happen to them. Naturally, I dressed up as a clown and joined her for one day.

Anyway, I really appreciate you a whole lot. I hope to get to know you even better from here on out! Seriously. Don't be afraid to contact me at the below information. xo.

Sincerely,
Austin James Robinson

Harvey Li,

If you're reading this, it's because you 'liked' or 'reacted' to a Facebook status I made back in April. I know, it's been awhile and I suck! I expect you to expect me to send you the Cheesecake Factory Menu or something – and honestly I will do that at a later time if you wish, – but this is a letter containing things I appreciate about you.

1). Okay, so as I was scavenging your Facebook page, I realized that I actually don't really know you that well. Like, at all. I'm glad to see you're very dedicated to the Chinese Student Association, but unfortunately we do not share that connection, so I cannot say much about it. I would make up stuff based on what I've found, but I'd rather get to know you better and then hopefully be able to warrant a 250-word letter about what I appreciate about you. But for now, maybe you can help me with this:

2). So, back in 6th grade, I had this best friend named Cassie Boyd. At the end of the year, she moved away, not telling anyone where she was headed. We didn't even know she had plans to move away – we just didn't see her the next year. Anyway, it's been, like, 11 years now and me and a couple of other classmates have tried our hardest to find her on the World Wide Web to no avail. What are we to do? Should we create a website dedicated to trying to find her? www.whereiscassieboyd.com, perhaps? I miss her.

Anyway, I really appreciate you a whole lot. I hope to get to know you even better from here on out! Seriously. Don't be afraid to contact me at the below information. xo.

Sincerely,
Austin James Robinson

PROJECT LETTERS

Hasan Tinwala,

If you're reading this, it's because you 'liked' or 'reacted' to a Facebook status I made back in April. I know, it's been awhile and I suck! I expect you to expect me to send you the Cheesecake Factory Menu or something – and honestly I will do that at a later time if you wish, – but this is a letter containing things I appreciate about you.

1). Your dedication to Senate of College Councils and making the campus a better place for every Longhorn (and, thus, the world a better place for every human). I met you in the Senate office, if I'm not mistaken, and I believe you are still heavily involved (I don't go to UT anymore, so just yell at me if this is not true). Not only have you simply been in Senate, which is already incredible, but also you really put your heart and sweat into the organization. It's incredible how dedicated you are to ensuring that the academic culture at UT remain great.

2). How blunt you are. Remember when you told me to get rid of my neckbeard? LMAO. I guess this could be seen as a bad thing in a sense, but at least you were willing to say it out loud (whereas, I'm pretty sure everyone else in that office was just thinking it and wasn't going to notify me). Being truthful and honest is always the way to go, in my opinion, so thanks for that :P

Anyway, I really appreciate you a whole lot. I hope to get to know you even better from here on out! Seriously. Don't be afraid to contact me at the below information. xo.

Sincerely,
Austin James Robinson

[NAME REDACTED],

If you're reading this, it's because you 'liked' or 'reacted' to a Facebook status I made back in April. I know, it's been awhile and I suck! I expect you to expect me to send you the Cheesecake Factory Menu or something – and honestly I will do that at a later time if you wish, – but this is a letter containing things I appreciate about you.

1). Omg, I can't believe you liked this considering I met you literally once because of [REDACTED]. I LOVE IT. I'm so glad you liked it. However, it's unfortunate because I literally don't really know you and, thus, cannot think of an entire letter of good things to write for you. But here's a cool story about the time I scammed a boy into going out with me:

2). So I was in 9th grade and I walked into the local grocery store. I saw this really cute guy. He was bagging the groceries because he worked there. So I decided to buy something (I wasn't going to originally because I was a hoodlum who loitered around grocery stores back then apparently). I picked up a literal potato and went to the cashier. I asked them to bag just that single potato because I really wanted that cute guy to bag my potato. It even sounds hot, right! Anyway, we started dating a couple weeks later and then he cheated on me. Isn't that awesome!

3). Also, you're really hot.

Anyway, I really appreciate you a whole lot. I hope to get to know you even better from here on out! Seriously. Don't be afraid to contact me at the below information. xo.

Sincerely,
Austin James Robinson

Hasnain Bherwani,

If you're reading this, it's because you 'liked' or 'reacted' to a Facebook status I made back in April. I know, it's been awhile and I suck! I expect you to expect me to send you the Cheesecake Factory Menu or something – and honestly I will do that at a later time if you wish, – but this is a letter containing things I appreciate about you.

1). Your sense of humor. Honestly, dude, this is the only thing I know about you. But I'm glad I know it about you. You are incredibly funny, and I feel like we'd really enjoy being around each other if we ever met in person. But anyway, considering that's never happened, I can't really write you a 250-word letter about what I appreciate about you. However, I can tell you a story about the time I sort-of got conned into going to Amsterdam for a week by myself.

2). So I use this popular Jewish dating app because I'm a lonely boy! It was all fun and games until I matched with this guy in New York City who had a super minor part on Orange Is The New Black. Cool! Yeah, that's what I thought. He said he was starring in a new film that was airing at the Rotterdam International Film Festival in the Netherlands, and that he wanted me to go with him. Cool! I want to stop here to state that I know with 100% certainty that this guy was not catfishing me. Anyway, I buy a plane ticket and get everything done. A couple weeks before the event, he tells me that he not only doesn't want to go anymore, but he also doesn't want to speak to me anymore. Literally out of NOWHERE. Kind of iconic, right? Like rude, but iconic. Anyway, I go to the Netherlands anyway. I stay seven days in Amsterdam. And I even go see his movie at the film festival in Rotterdam. (Spoiler Alert: he dies first.)

Anyway, I really appreciate you a whole lot. I hope to

get to know you even better from here on out! Seriously. Don't be afraid to contact me at the below information. xo.

Sincerely,
Austin James Robinson

Heath Fowler,

If you're reading this, it's because you 'liked' or 'reacted' to a Facebook status I made back in April. I know, it's been awhile and I suck! I expect you to expect me to send you the Cheesecake Factory Menu or something – and honestly I will do that at a later time if you wish, – but this is a letter containing things I appreciate about you.

1). Ahhhh, shit. I really don't know where I'm going to start with you. I guess let's talk about how I'm pretty sure you're the funniest person I know (literally) and how I think you could successfully create a social media comedy empire if you truly tried. I mean, you need to get it together with that This Hiss Madagascar Hissing Cockroaches vlog. You're beginning to really drop the ball on that. This is where you could get your start in online questionable comedy! I look forward to it.

2). How we took a road trip around the United States that one time but we were really supposed to go to Canada but then last minute you told me that you didn't have a passport? Do you remember that? As long as you do, then we're good. If not, then we're going to have to do it all over again. Sorry everyone involved!

3). Remember when I used to have a crush on you? That was icky and gross and I don't know what I was doing at that point in my life! Sorry!

Anyway, I really appreciate you a whole lot. I hope to get to know you even better from here on out! Seriously. Don't be afraid to contact me at the below information. xo.

Sincerely,
Austin James Robinson

Heather Allison,

If you're reading this, it's because you 'liked' or 'reacted' to a Facebook status I made back in April. I know, it's been awhile and I suck! I expect you to expect me to send you the Cheesecake Factory Menu or something – and honestly I will do that at a later time if you wish, – but this is a letter containing things I appreciate about you.

1). The fact that we met at Hugh O'Brian Youth Leadership! I'm glad we could connect there and stay friends online! Although, I obviously have to admit that I don't believe we know each other *that well*, so hopefully we get to know each other better in the future! I hope you're continuing to volunteer with HOBY!! In the meantime, here's something I've been thinking about:

2). Okay, so you know how time zones are a thing? Well, imagine living on the edge of two different time zones. This is my dream because that means I will be able to eat at my favorite restaurant or fast food establishment, AND THEN I will be able to hop over to the earlier time zone and be able to eat again even though the later time zone's restaurant is CLOSED for the day. Like, talk about cheating the construct of time and capitalism, am I right?

Anyway, I really appreciate you a whole lot. I hope to get to know you even better from here on out! Seriously. Don't be afraid to contact me at the below information. xo.

Sincerely,
Austin James Robinson

Huey Rey Fischer,

If you're reading this, it's because you 'liked' or 'reacted' to a Facebook status I made back in April. I know, it's been awhile and I suck! I expect you to expect me to send you the Cheesecake Factory Menu or something – and honestly I will do that at a later time if you wish, – but this is a letter containing things I appreciate about you.

1). **The fact that you ran for a fucking political position. What the HELL. And I'm surprised you didn't win. I felt like every Longhorn was incredibly impressed and in awe at the fact that someone not much older than them (and who was in their shoes literally a couple years prior) was running for an elected position for the Texas Government. That was incredibly iconic, and I can't even imagine doing that at any point in my life, let alone in my early 20s.**

2). How funny you are. Idk not a lot of people are funny, so when I find someone who is actually funny (in my opinion), I appreciate them, like, way more than anyone else in my life. I honestly think you could be a comedian – not that you ever would want to be because I feel like your entire life aspiration is to help others and not act like a fool on stage – but I could see you being successful if you wanted.

3). That one time that we went to a drag show together and you (and the rest of our party) literally left me there because a guy was "flirting" with me and you wanted to give me some alone time with him. And then nothing ended up happening because of it hahaha. Ha. Ha-ha. Ha.

4). How everyone automatically feels obligated to say all three of your names together. Because, same. Sorry you can't have a cool acronym for your name like me (HRF just doesn't sound the same as AJR), but regardless: if someone doesn't say your full name,

they're wrong and you don't have to answer to them.

Anyway, I really appreciate you a whole lot. I hope to get to know you even better from here on out! Seriously. Don't be afraid to contact me at the below information. xo.

Sincerely,
Austin James Robinson

Ian Durben,

If you're reading this, it's because you 'liked' or 'reacted' to a Facebook status I made back in April. I know, it's been awhile and I suck! I expect you to expect me to send you the Cheesecake Factory Menu or something – and honestly I will do that at a later time if you wish, – but this is a letter containing things I appreciate about you.

1). Your sense of humor. You make me laugh so freaking much, and we haven't even spent that much time together at all. Like, we need to hang out more. I want to take all of the funny Texas Blazers and put them all in one room and see what jokes we can create / if we'll all explode.

2). The fact that you shaved your beautiful, BEAUTIFUL hair (like, literally amazing hair) in order to raise awareness and funds for cancer research. I almost cried (I don't cry, so this is a big deal). And your mother was so funny and amazing when I met her at that event (and when she said, "THEY DIDN'T GIVE YOU SUNSCREEN??" I laughed so hard). I can't wait to see how long it takes you to grow it back out. You look great either way.

3). HOW I DON'T KNOW YOUR MIDDLE NAME AND YOU WON'T TELL ME. I guess it's a running joke at this point, so I truly hope I never discover your middle name. Let's keep up the mystery.

Anyway, I really appreciate you a whole lot. I hope to get to know you even better from here on out! Seriously. Don't be afraid to contact me at the below information. xo.

Sincerely,
Austin James Robinson

Isaac Becker,

If you're reading this, it's because you 'liked' or 'reacted' to a Facebook status I made back in April. I know, it's been awhile and I suck! I expect you to expect me to send you the Cheesecake Factory Menu or something – and honestly I will do that at a later time if you wish, – but this is a letter containing things I appreciate about you.

1). How we became friends because of the PC Music forums and now we sort of talk about other things more than PC Music. Also, is that even still a music collective? I don't keep up with them much anymore. Anyway, Month of Mayhem who?

2). The fact that we physically met at a PC Music concert in a city that neither of us live in. That was a very fun time – even if I literally just sort of talked shit about PC Music in my previous point. Amazing experience, regardless. Let's do it again sometime!

3). The fact that we send jokes to each other all of the time, and basically nothing else at all. Let's keep it that way forever. Wait, let's actually make dumb-ass social media jokes together. I feel like we could both do really well with that if we teamed up.

Anyway, I really appreciate you a whole lot. I hope to get to know you even better from here on out! Seriously. Don't be afraid to contact me at the below information. xo.

Sincerely,
Austin James Robinson

Jack Maloney,

If you're reading this, it's because you 'liked' or 'reacted' to a Facebook status I made back in April. I know, it's been awhile and I suck! I expect you to expect me to send you the Cheesecake Factory Menu or something – and honestly I will do that at a later time if you wish, – but this is a letter containing things I appreciate about you.

1). How every time I go to Arizona, I basically see you and Max and Jake and everyone else (I'm done trying to name everyone). TUCSON BOYS. We've had some great adventures in Tucson, a city that a lot of people take for granted. I find it incredibly beautiful and mountainous. THANKS.

2). The fact that you're in my faux boy band named after me. We all need to do another photo-shoot together. Maybe even make a really terrible song that no one likes. The possibilities are endless. Thank you for taking this journey with me.

3). Your sense of humor and your personality. You're weird as fuck – we all know that. But your humor is very unique and I love it. Whether we're eating 14 meals for, like, $2 at Waffle House, making a ruckus at Applebee's, or just annoying the hell out of Max, you're always FUNNY and COOL. WOW.

Anyway, I really appreciate you a whole lot. I hope to get to know you even better from here on out! Seriously. Don't be afraid to contact me at the below information. xo.

Sincerely,
Austin James Robinson

Jacob Merrill,

If you're reading this, it's because you 'liked' or 'reacted' to a Facebook status I made back in April. I know, it's been awhile and I suck! I expect you to expect me to send you the Cheesecake Factory Menu or something – and honestly I will do that at a later time if you wish, – but this is a letter containing things I appreciate about you.

1). Okay, you know what: I'm literally going to copy and paste what I wrote for Jack because how the hell are you two different people?

2). How every time I go to Arizona, I basically see you and Max and Jake and everyone else (I'm done trying to name everyone). TUCSON BOYS. We've had some great adventures in Tucson, a city that a lot of people take for granted. I find it incredibly beautiful and mountainous. THANKS.

3). The fact that you're in my faux boy band named after me. We all need to do another photoshoot together. Maybe even make a really terrible song that no one likes. The possibilities are endless. Thank you for taking this journey with me.

4). Your sense of humor and your personality. You're weird as fuck – we all know that. But your humor is very unique and I love it. Whether we're eating 14 meals for, like, $2 at Waffle House, making a ruckus at Applebee's, or just annoying the hell out of Max, you're always FUNNY and COOL. WOW.

Anyway, I really appreciate you a whole lot. I hope to get to know you even better from here on out! Seriously. Don't be afraid to contact me at the below information. xo.

Sincerely,
Austin James Robinson

PROJECT LETTERS

Jake Sacks,

If you're reading this, it's because you 'liked' or 'reacted' to a Facebook status I made back in April. I know, it's been awhile and I suck! I expect you to expect me to send you the Cheesecake Factory Menu or something – and honestly I will do that at a later time if you wish, – but this is a letter containing things I appreciate about you.

1). Everything. Idk, it's going to be really freaking hard for me to make a list for you because I legitimately appreciate everything about you. You know you mean too much to me, and I'm not sure where to start. Okay, this was a bad first point.

2). The fact that I feel like I know your entire family now?? Well, at least your immediate family. I love that. I feel like friends in college never get to meet each others family members, and I just love that I have met a good chunk of yours. And the Judaism is a plus. I mean, whatttttt.

3). Your ability to initiate self-growth and constantly think in depth about your life. I know you're having constant struggles about finishing your PhD, along with making music. And I know it doesn't make it easy when you're also struggling with anxiety and depression. But I love how open you are to me about all of it, and how you think about all of it in constructive ways – and allow other people to give you feedback about it all in order for you to take it into consideration. You're doing great.

Anyway, I really appreciate you a whole lot. I hope to get to know you even better from here on out! Seriously. Don't be afraid to contact me at the below information. xo.

Sincerely,
Austin James Robinson

James Cimino,

If you're reading this, it's because you 'liked' or 'reacted' to a Facebook status I made back in April. I know, it's been awhile and I suck! I expect you to expect me to send you the Cheesecake Factory Menu or something – and honestly I will do that at a later time if you wish, – but this is a letter containing things I appreciate about you.

1). The fact that you're super buff, but also basically a small puppy. You could probably basically kill me with one arm tied behind your back, but you could also hug me with one arm tied behind your back. You are incredibly sweet and caring to everyone in your life, and I know that's your true personality. You just also happen to be buff, and don't hold many of the stereotypes that come along with guys who are fit. God bless.

2). How you're in THE MARINES??? What the HECK. Not only that, but you became an officer in the Marines directly after graduating university. You're amazing. I love that about you so much because, as we've discussed before, I want to be in the Air Force (so wayyyyyy different than the Marines, but still in the military, so we're going there) and you were one of the only people I could talk to about it at the time that we did. A lot of people have these awfully negative stigmas toward the military, and the only thing I've really gotten back from anyone at the university / in Texas Blazers (except for from you) has been, "Oh, well the military is highly problematic." Not even helpful or anything. So, you are a blessing in my life.

Anyway, I really appreciate you a whole lot. I hope to get to know you even better from here on out! Seriously. Don't be afraid to contact me at the below information. xo.

Sincerely,
Austin James Robinson

PROJECT LETTERS

James Fisk,

If you're reading this, it's because you 'liked' or 'reacted' to a Facebook status I made back in April. I know, it's been awhile and I suck! I expect you to expect me to send you the Cheesecake Factory Menu or something – and honestly I will do that at a later time if you wish, – but this is a letter containing things I appreciate about you.

1). How I had a crush on you for, like, two full years and refused to talk to you because of that. Before we actually became friends, I feel like I definitely just had a crush on you from the background and lived through [REDACTED] to hear about you. I was really freaking creepy about all of that. And I remember that one time we finally met at The Q (while watching RuPaul's Drag Race) and I sort of just hit on you and then ran away and left? Idk, that was a weird time for me. I'm sorry for literally ALL of that.

2). That time we hung out in Albuquerque and went to a Savers. I actually composed myself pretty well in those moments, considering they were directly after I was kind of obsessed with you. But yeah, that was a super fun time and made me realize how truly funny you are in everyday situations. Cool!

3). The fact that you left me at a drag show so that I could flirt with a guy I was never going to get. Yeah, remember that? It was you and your boyfriend and Huey and his boyfriend and then just me as a 5th wheel (yay). And y'all ALL LEFT ME AT THE DRAG SHOW SOLELY SO I COULD SOMEHOW GET A BOYFRIEND (we all knew it wasn't going to happen). That was kind of sweet though.

Anyway, I really appreciate you a whole lot. I hope to get to know you even better from here on out! Seriously. Don't be afraid to contact me at the below information. xo.

Sincerely,
Austin James Robinson

Jasleen Shokar,

If you're reading this, it's because you 'liked' or 'reacted' to a Facebook status I made back in April. I know, it's been awhile and I suck! I expect you to expect me to send you the Cheesecake Factory Menu or something – and honestly I will do that at a later time if you wish, – but this is a letter containing things I appreciate about you.

1). How dedicated you are to Senate of College Councils and Student Government, and the University of Texas in general! You have done SO much for the university, the students, and – I'll say it, – the world. Never stop being fully dedicated to the things and causes that you believe in. Serving others is contagious, and you sure make me wish I was doing more!

2). How much you love Beyoncé. I'm pretty sure even if Beyoncé ONLY had you as a fan, she'd still be just as famous. That's how BIG your love for her is. Inspiring! I'm glad she could change your life, and I hope she realizes one day that you are absolutely her biggest fan and that she needs to name an entire album after you.

3). That time that me, you, Stewart, and Seth ate brunch in El Paso. Iconic. That's all I need to say about THAT.

Anyway, I really appreciate you a whole lot. I hope to get to know you even better from here on out! Seriously. Don't be afraid to contact me at the below information. xo.

Sincerely,
Austin James Robinson

PROJECT LETTERS

Jason Thompson,

If you're reading this, it's because you 'liked' or 'reacted' to a Facebook status I made back in April. I know, it's been awhile and I suck! I expect you to expect me to send you the Cheesecake Factory Menu or something – and honestly I will do that at a later time if you wish, – but this is a letter containing things I appreciate about you.

1). How often you suggest new t-shirt ideas to me. I don't know if you remember this, but you have asked me to make a t-shirt at least two different times. You asked me to make one that says, "GO FUCK YOURSELF SAN DIEGO" and one that says, "JASON MUTHA FUCKIN' THOMPSON" – both very good ideas, and I apologize for never creating them. To my defense, the t-shirt shop I use does not allow cursing on their products (I know – they SUCK), so there was no way I was going to be able to make you those shirts. But someday!

2). The fact that you look fucking hot with both long hair and short hair. Yeah, you joined APO with long-ass hair and it was really cool and you were really cool. And you're still really cool! So I guess your personality isn't solely in your hair is what we've all learned here. Amen.

3). Anyway, wtf, we need to catch up and actually talk and update each other on lives and whatnot. I feel like we haven't *really* talked since, like, pledge semester back in 2014. Not that we've ever been great friends or anything, but I believe you did used to live, like, in the same building as me at Town Lake. What the heck!

Anyway, I really appreciate you a whole lot. I hope to get to know you even better from here on out! Seriously. Don't be afraid to contact me at the below information. xo.

Sincerely,
Austin James Robinson

Jay Patel,

If you're reading this, it's because you 'liked' or 'reacted' to a Facebook status I made back in April. I know, it's been awhile and I suck! I expect you to expect me to send you the Cheesecake Factory Menu or something – and honestly I will do that at a later time if you wish, – but this is a letter containing things I appreciate about you.

1). The fact that you've always supported me and my weird brand and all of the dumb shit that I do. I'm so glad to have people like you in my life because literally you're the only reason I continue to push out the stupidestestest content imaginable. Yay!

2). How you whole-heartedly supported my Student Government Executive Alliance campaign even though you weren't even a student. Remember when we had that lunch at Taco Joint in order to discuss it all? I miss times like those. I hope we have opportunities to hang out in the future. I will literally force you to hang out with me if you decline.

3). You're fucking funny, dude. And hella smart. It's like a dangerous combination. Oh also you're pretty hot. So, just keep doing those things, I guess!

Anyway, I really appreciate you a whole lot. I hope to get to know you even better from here on out! Seriously. Don't be afraid to contact me at the below information. xo.

Sincerely,
Austin James Robinson

PROJECT LETTERS

Jay Wilk,

If you're reading this, it's because you 'liked' or 'reacted' to a Facebook status I made back in April. I know, it's been awhile and I suck! I expect you to expect me to send you the Cheesecake Factory Menu or something – and honestly I will do that at a later time if you wish, – but this is a letter containing things I appreciate about you.

1). Okay okay okay, where to start. OH – the fact that you were basically everyone's guardian while in Paris (and really everywhere else in Europe). You booked EVERYTHING for EVERYONE when we went to Paris, and basically made sure everyone was good and that our AirBNB reservation checked out and we weren't going to die, and all that good stuff. And you basically did that for every place we went to. I don't know if everyone expressed appreciation for that, but trust me: we were all hella grateful to have someone like you. The rest of us are basically small babies.

2). How in love with LUSH you are! And your ability to get everyone else to catch the LUSH bug. I don't even think I knew what LUSH was before you took me to the flagship store in London. And now I literally take pictures of LUSH stores all across the country. And I go in and try new things. I was never even into beauty / care products before you! You're gonna own LUSH one day.

3). How dedicated you are to intersectional equality and advocating for the rights of EVERYONE. It's truly iconic. You aren't afraid to call people out, and then have a discussion with them so they understand further (you've definitely done this with me a few times). Keep doing it!

Anyway, I really appreciate you a whole lot. I hope to get to know you even better from here on out! Seriously. Don't be afraid to contact me at the below information. xo.

Sincerely,
Austin James Robinson

JC Rudy,

If you're reading this, it's because you 'liked' or 'reacted' to a Facebook status I made back in April. I know, it's been awhile and I suck! I expect you to expect me to send you the Cheesecake Factory Menu or something – and honestly I will do that at a later time if you wish, – but this is a letter containing things I appreciate about you.

1). How dedicated you are / were to Alpha Phi Omega (honestly I have no clue who's still in it). I remember pledging with you and doing a majority of the service events with you. It was basically me and you who did, like, everything in regard to service and volunteering in our pledge class. We were wild af – I have no clue how we were even able to do that much. Literally looking back, I must have made my life entirely APO-related because got dang: we were like MACHINES. Kind of glad I got out of that grind work and found my niche when it comes to volunteering.

2). The fact that you're in the Rocky Horror Picture Show at the Alamo! I think it's called The Queerio's, but then I think the name also changed. Who can never be sure? I went to one of y'all's showings and it was absolutely amazing. [REDACTED] had her boobs out and totally sat on my lap during the performance. Iconic. And of course, you were amazing, too. I hope you're still doing that!

Anyway, I really appreciate you a whole lot. I hope to get to know you even better from here on out! Seriously. Don't be afraid to contact me at the below information. xo.

Sincerely,
Austin James Robinson

[NAME REDACTED],

If you're reading this, it's because you 'liked' or 'reacted' to a Facebook status I made back in April. I know, it's been awhile and I suck! I expect you to expect me to send you the Cheesecake Factory Menu or something – and honestly I will do that at a later time if you wish, – but this is a letter containing things I appreciate about you.

1). How dedicated you were to [REDACTED]. I mean, I wasn't in [REDACTED] that long (I think, like, 3 semesters), but I always remember you being there, and everyone enjoying you and your humor.

2). How I discovered weird (AKA good) equestrian-girl running competitions because of you. Idk what is even happening, but all I know is that one day I was scrolling through Facebook minding my own business and then I see this girl running on all fours and jumping over hurdles like a GOT DANG HORSE. That changed my life, so thank you for changing my life.

3). That one time I was on a rooftop because of an [REDACTED] party and completely hit on your boyfriend (okay, I'm not sure if he's still your boyfriend or not so I hope this letter doesn't turn out to be a complete FLOP). You were cool about it. It was all fine. We're al doing fine. Whatever.

Anyway, I really appreciate you a whole lot. I hope to get to know you even better from here on out! Seriously. Don't be afraid to contact me at the below information. xo.

Sincerely,
Austin James Robinson

[NAME REDACTED],

If you're reading this, it's because you 'liked' or 'reacted' to a Facebook status I made back in April. I know, it's been awhile and I suck! I expect you to expect me to send you the Cheesecake Factory Menu or something – and honestly I will do that at a later time if you wish, – but this is a letter containing things I appreciate about you.

1). Okay, so we don't really know each other that well at all, so instead of pretending to know you by going through your Facebook and throwing bullshit together, I'll just talk about something we both know about: [REDACTED].

2). I know you're also into politics, so I was just wondering if you knew about / have any opinions on the current Texas Bills [REDACTED] and [REDACTED] regarding [REDACTED]. Like, it sounds great, right? (Plus, some of those places seem like sweatshops anyway.) However, the CEO of my company [REDACTED] and basically everyone here believe that if these bills were to pass, it would basically give less work and working times to [REDACTED] considering they'd be [REDACTED]. Thus, they'd have nothing to do for the rest of the day, and many times [REDACTED]. So, anyway, I'm not stating my opinion or stance in this, but it's just a realllllllly interesting debate. And just curious if you want to talk about this!

Anyway, I really appreciate you a whole lot. I hope to get to know you even better from here on out! Seriously. Don't be afraid to contact me at the below information. xo.

Sincerely,
Austin James Robinson

Jessica Gomez,

If you're reading this, it's because you 'liked' or 'reacted' to a Facebook status I made back in April. I know, it's been awhile and I suck! I expect you to expect me to send you the Cheesecake Factory Menu or something – and honestly I will do that at a later time if you wish, – but this is a letter containing things I appreciate about you.

1). The fact that we did Extreme Youth Leadership together!!! I miss those days – they were so long ago. I only ever volunteered there one year after my camp year, but I hope you stayed! If not, oh well! At least we got to meet! Although, we don't really know each other that well, so I won't be able to say more about you than what I've already said ☹ But do you want to know how close I am to getting to personally know Mitchell Musso?

2). So, at another leadership camp I volunteered at, Mitchell Musso's cousin attended. No one knew he was the Hannah Montana star's cousin, but his last name was Musso and I jokingly said, "Haha – are you related to Mitchell Musso or something?" He sincerely said, "Yes," and then showed me proof of him on set of Hannah Montana. Isn't that crazy? Anyway, now I'm Facebook friends with Mason Musso – one half of Metro Station – somehow. I don't know where I'm going with this.

Anyway, I really appreciate you a whole lot. I hope to get to know you even better from here on out! Seriously. Don't be afraid to contact me at the below information. xo.

Sincerely,
Austin James Robinson

Jim Hampton,

If you're reading this, it's because you 'liked' or 'reacted' to a Facebook status I made back in April. I know, it's been awhile and I suck! I expect you to expect me to send you the Cheesecake Factory Menu or something – and honestly I will do that at a later time if you wish, – but this is a letter containing things I appreciate about you.

1). Your BAND. Boys Club SUCKS, and it is also one of the best local bands I have ever heard. And I'm being completely sincere about that. I wish I wasn't because I hate you! But the truth is, the band is good and you are good.

2). Your Twitter, or your sense of humor. From memes to just plain good writing, you are a really humorous person. I could see you as a comedian. You should be a comedian! Wow I can't believe I just decided your life goal for you – you're welcome.

3). That one time you took to Twitter to tell all of us that you will write a poem based on any tweet that we send you. That's such a cool project. Were those ever going to be public? Understandable if not, but I have this one friend who won't stop asking me when he's gonna get his poem LMAO.

4). The fact that you were a good sport when I got drunk that one time and kept calling you hot. Amen.

Anyway, I really appreciate you a whole lot. I hope to get to know you even better from here on out! Seriously. Don't be afraid to contact me at the below information. xo.

Sincerely,
Austin James Robinson

Jimmy Yoder,

If you're reading this, it's because you 'liked' or 'reacted' to a Facebook status I made back in April. I know, it's been awhile and I suck! I expect you to expect me to send you the Cheesecake Factory Menu or something – and honestly I will do that at a later time if you wish, – but this is a letter containing things I appreciate about you.

1). Your kindness. Okay, you literally blew me away when I was on the selection committee your new guy year. I knew I wanted you in immediately because you're just such a genuinely kind guy, and I love that. I believe you stated something about always being nice and not mean (okay, I probably butchered anything you ever could have possibly said regarding kindness, but you get what I mean), and my biggest goal in life is to be nice – and my favorite trait in other people is kindness. Anyway, I'm ranting, but I'm just in love with you oKAY.

2). Your humor. I love your Twitter so much because you are so hilarious with your retweets and your own tweets. I want you to personally tattoo them onto me. Let's set up a time to do this.

3). THE TIME WE WENT TO THAT SMOOTHIE PLACE AND SAID WE'D TOTALLY GO THERE FIVE MORE TIMES, BUT DIDN'T. Honestly, I love how all of that went down, even the fact that we never went back. I think that totally speaks volumes about our friendship, and that's what I've always loved about us. What am I even saying at this point?

Anyway, I really appreciate you a whole lot. I hope to get to know you even better from here on out! Seriously. Don't be afraid to contact me at the below information. xo.

Sincerely,
Austin James Robinson

Joe Bowman,

If you're reading this, it's because you 'liked' or 'reacted' to a Facebook status I made back in April. I know, it's been awhile and I suck! I expect you to expect me to send you the Cheesecake Factory Menu or something – and honestly I will do that at a later time if you wish, – but this is a letter containing things I appreciate about you.

1). The fact that you were – quite literally – the coolest person I ever met in Liberal Arts Council. Okay, LAC was filled with a bunch of dickweeds and gross, pretentious people. That's honestly why I only lasted a year in there. Anyway, this is beside the point – you were pretty fucking cool. We had some amazing conversations, and I'm happy I was apart of that organization if only because I got to meet you. Continue being the only cool person in whatever you do!

2). How you're totally in the music industry in LA now, apparently??? You're the definition of iconic and someone who goes after his dreams. I could never. I should, but I don't have the guts you have, apparently. But maybe I'll make it to LA one day and we'll rekindle our friendship. You'll have to update me on all of the cool stuff you do over there. And let me know if I can ever help you with anything ever. Literally.

Anyway, I really appreciate you a whole lot. I hope to get to know you even better from here on out! Seriously. Don't be afraid to contact me at the below information. xo.

Sincerely,
Austin James Robinson

[NAME REDACTED],

If you're reading this, it's because you 'liked' or 'reacted' to a Facebook status I made back in April. I know, it's been awhile and I suck! I expect you to expect me to send you the Cheesecake Factory Menu or something – and honestly I will do that at a later time if you wish, – but this is a letter containing things I appreciate about you.

1). How supportive you were when me and Daniel were running for Student Government Executive Alliance. That means so much to me because we were definitely the smallest campaign running and had, like, 1/4th of the people the other campaigns had (if not wayyyyy less than the two front-running campaigns). You were willing to update all of your photos and post about us, which is honestly what the election is all about anyway (unfortunately). Thank you so much for your support!!

2). The fact that we met because of [REDACTED] even though I'm not even in that [REDACTED], and really don't like many people in it. But you're pretty cool and I enjoy you a lot. I always get you mixed up with [REDACTED], so there's that. You're cooler though (I hope he sees this, because I'm probably going to tell him that he's cooler than you).

Anyway, I really appreciate you a whole lot. I hope to get to know you even better from here on out! Seriously. Don't be afraid to contact me at the below information. xo.

Sincerely,
Austin James Robinson

Jordan Shafer,

If you're reading this, it's because you 'liked' or 'reacted' to a Facebook status I made back in April. I know, it's been awhile and I suck! I expect you to expect me to send you the Cheesecake Factory Menu or something – and honestly I will do that at a later time if you wish, – but this is a letter containing things I appreciate about you.

1). How you listen to GOOD music. I think one of the first things we ever bonded over was the fact that we're both into a wide variety of music that doesn't necessarily make it to the radio. Like Sufjan Stevens and Goodbyetomorrow and stuff like that. Actually, one of the ONLY playlist I've made on my iTunes is just called "Jordan Shafer" lmao.

2). How you're my little in Alpha Phi Omega and totally fit in with the rest. Literally all of you are so weird and somehow it actually feels like a family. In all of my other organizations, the littles don't really talk to each other and half of the time I don't feel like I relate to them at all. But for some reason all of you in APO fit together. So thanks for being cool.

3). The fact that you created a stamp with my name on it. I still use it. It's literally sitting on my work desk right now. I haven't started signing things with it because I feel like that would make my boss mad, but I will SOON.

4). That time you were super drunk on a roof and I offered you chicken crispers from Chili's and you literally looked at them and said, "These aren't chicken crispers!" even though they were. Amen.

Anyway, I really appreciate you a whole lot. I hope to get to know you even better from here on out! Seriously. Don't be afraid to contact me at the below information. xo.

Sincerely,
Austin James Robinson

Joseph Bae,

If you're reading this, it's because you 'liked' or 'reacted' to a Facebook status I made back in April. I know, it's been awhile and I suck! I expect you to expect me to send you the Cheesecake Factory Menu or something – and honestly I will do that at a later time if you wish, – but this is a letter containing things I appreciate about you.

1). Your last name. I mean, I know you get this a lot, so I'm sorry if this entire letter is now off-putting because I started with this. But I remember first seeing your name (for some reason – I think I had your email address or something) and thinking, "What a name." Then before I knew it, we were online friends.

2). How dedicated to organizations you are and how popular you are. I'm pretty sure everyone knows who you are. I feel like I know you because of the Kevin / Binna campaign and Camp Texas people, among other things. And honestly, I'm not even sure if you were involved with either of those thing because I don't think we've ever personally talked before. Regardless, you must be dedicated to be known by all of these people.

3). The fact that you created that meme page. I'll admit: I HATE memes. And there are way too many normies and people who don't know how to joke at all in that page for me to be comfortable. But damn is it growing FAST. And I admire that you started it all.

Anyway, I really appreciate you a whole lot. I hope to get to know you even better from here on out! Seriously. Don't be afraid to contact me at the below information. xo.

Sincerely,
Austin James Robinson

Joseph Raff,

If you're reading this, it's because you 'liked' or 'reacted' to a Facebook status I made back in April. I know, it's been awhile and I suck! I expect you to expect me to send you the Cheesecake Factory Menu or something – and honestly I will do that at a later time if you wish, – but this is a letter containing things I appreciate about you.

1). **The time we met at HOBY and me, you, and E basically became this weird trio that made no sense. I miss those times so much. E eventually came back to volunteer with me, but where were you????? HUH. I haven't seen you since then and I miss you ☹ I will need to visit you wherever the hell you are now (I know it was Chicago, but I think you recently graduated). Let's plan that!**

2). **The fact that we have Stewart Schweinfurth as a mutual friend. Yes, this is enough to make me appreciate YOU even more (and also distracts you from the fact that I don't really have any other points to make in this letter). Stewart being our mutual friend is amazing, and is probably the only reason we met each other. I know that makes absolutely no sense, but just THINK about it. Okay, because of this really shitty point, I think we need to create more reasons to appreciate each other. Let's hang out again someday, please!**

Anyway, I really appreciate you a whole lot. I hope to get to know you even better from here on out! Seriously. Don't be afraid to contact me at the below information. xo.

Sincerely,
Austin James Robinson

PROJECT LETTERS

Joshua Richardson,

If you're reading this, it's because you 'liked' or 'reacted' to a Facebook status I made back in April. I know, it's been awhile and I suck! I expect you to expect me to send you the Cheesecake Factory Menu or something – and honestly I will do that at a later time if you wish, – but this is a letter containing things I appreciate about you.

1). Your hair. Idk, this is pretty self-explanatory and a really good reason. Enough said.

2). Your meme-abilities. I think people think of you instantly when they think of the UT Memes page (I don't even think of Joseph Bae before you). Likewise, before that, you were typically known for memes and your Facebook tomfoolery, in general. I know this definitely makes a lot of people happy, which is very much needed in a college environment. Thank GOD.

3). Your commitment to civic engagement. I first met you because of Student Government, which seems interesting considering we mainly post comedy on the interwebs and it seems we would have initially met some other way not related to being SERIOUSLY POLITICAL BOY (2002). Likewise, you're pretty into service and helping the world, in general. People who can simultaneously help the world and make memes are the future – for real. (Sorry you didn't receive my scholarship – I can give you the names and addresses of the people on the selection committee and you can doxx them.)

Anyway, I really appreciate you a whole lot. I hope to get to know you even better from here on out! Seriously. Don't be afraid to contact me at the below information. xo.

Sincerely,
Austin James Robinson

[NAME REDACTED],

If you're reading this, it's because you 'liked' or 'reacted' to a Facebook status I made back in April. I know, it's been awhile and I suck! I expect you to expect me to send you the Cheesecake Factory Menu or something – and honestly I will do that at a later time if you wish, – but this is a letter containing things I appreciate about you.

1). How nice you are. That sounds like a bullshit reason, but every time I've seen you on [REDACTED], you've immediately talked to me and you were extremely sweet and we were able to talk about whatever! I really like that in my friends. However, other than that, we really don't know each other that well at all. Definitely not enough where I can fill a 250-word letter with what I appreciate about you. So here's a story instead:

2). Do you ever buy mixtapes from those guys on the street in major cities? When I was in DC back in 2013, I interacted with my first "street rapper" who asked me to buy his mixtape. I was like, sure! It was actually pretty good – he remixed "Somebody That I Used To Know" by Gotye, and none of it was necessarily BAD. However, since then I have become obsessed with buying mixtapes in every major city that I go to. I have collected literally dozens of CDs sold on the street to me. And they're ALL bad! There was this one rapper named after a popular seasoning (I'm afraid he'll sue me if he sees this somehow), and he started all of his songs with, "Let me put some seasonin' on it!" Which, granted, is a great line. But his music just wasn't good! Regardless, each and every mixtape I have bought off of the streets was a gem and I would do it all over again.

Anyway, I really appreciate you a whole lot. I hope to get to know you even better from here on out! Seriously. Don't be afraid to contact me at the below information. xo.

Sincerely,
Austin James Robinson

PROJECT LETTERS

Justin Blake Robinson,

If you're reading this, it's because you 'liked' or 'reacted' to a Facebook status I made back in April. I know, it's been awhile and I suck! I expect you to expect me to send you the Cheesecake Factory Menu or something – and honestly I will do that at a later time if you wish, – but this is a letter containing things I appreciate about you.

1). Your dedication to gymnastics and cheerleading. Idk, I don't even know how to lift my leg or what an arm is. I can't believe you've become a 'cheerlebrity' – did you ever think that would happen in your life? Make the most out of it. Sell apparel or something. Write a book. Actually, literally write a book. Idk if anyone else in Cheerleading is even doing that right now. So maybe capitalize on that. I can totally ghostwrite it and publish it. And with your outreach, you could sell a bunch.

2). The fact that you and Chris are still together. I think my longest relationship lasted for a hot second, so that's pretty cool that you've found someone who you'll probably marry or something. (What do people do nowadays? Is marriage still a thing?) Also he's really cool. I like him a whole lot and I really do want to call him my brother-in-law one day because not only is he cool, but his entire family is really cool. Even his mother.

3). Your sense of humor. We have at least a slither of similar joke styles. I feel like Robbie is going to be a little shit who won't understand comedy – so at least we have this.

Anyway, I really appreciate you a whole lot. I hope to get to know you even better from here on out! Seriously. Don't be afraid to contact me at the below information. xo.

Sincerely,
Austin James Robinson

Kali Stanley,

If you're reading this, it's because you 'liked' or 'reacted' to a Facebook status I made back in April. I know, it's been awhile and I suck! I expect you to expect me to send you the Cheesecake Factory Menu or something – and honestly I will do that at a later time if you wish, – but this is a letter containing things I appreciate about you.

1). How you're really funny and I like to think I'm really funny, but we don't know each other that well. Why aren't we better friends? We could make each other laugh or maybe you could make me laugh and I could just sit there?? I really don't know that much about you at all, and that makes me sad. So much, that I'm not sure I can continue this letter making you believe I know enough about you to write 250-words. So I'm going to tell you a story about the time I got a sexually transmitted infection without even having sex!

2). Okay, so I know crabs can hardly be considered an "infection" – but it's still an STI and apparently it's the only one you can get without being intimate with another human being. In my case, I was intimate with a bed, because I like to sleep. Apparently when someone has crabs, the beds they sleep on can hold crabs for up to three weeks afterwards. That's right! When you stay literally anywhere that isn't your own bed, you are at risk of getting an STI! Isn't that fun? So, yeah, I got crabs because I traveled the US the summer of 2015. And that was the best part of that summer.

Anyway, I really appreciate you a whole lot. I hope to get to know you even better from here on out! Seriously. Don't be afraid to contact me at the below information. xo.

Sincerely,
Austin James Robinson

PROJECT LETTERS

Kat Agudo,

If you're reading this, it's because you 'liked' or 'reacted' to a Facebook status I made back in April. I know, it's been awhile and I suck! I expect you to expect me to send you the Cheesecake Factory Menu or something – and honestly I will do that at a later time if you wish, – but this is a letter containing things I appreciate about you.

1). How we met. Do you remember how we met? I was inside of a tent attempting comedy and trying to win a Student Government Executive Alliance election, and you came up to our tent and got inside in order to ask us what the hell we were doing. I still can't answer that to this day, but you seemed really cool and I'm glad we're still friends. Although, I don't know too much about you. So instead of being really fake and pretending like I appreciate the hell out of you, I'm going to tell you about my YouTube videos and how I think I'm really hitting a kink goldmine on accident.

2). Back in 2010, I uploaded a YouTube video of me shaving my armpits. This was just an attempt to create "weird" content and act like I was cool. But apparently that's a kink people have? Watching people shave their armpits on YouTube? And it got a lot of views and I thought it was for ME – but they really just wanted my freaking armpits!!! Throughout the years, I continued uploading similar content like washing my feet or pretending to be trapped in a bathroom for 15-hours straight. And I guess people just really like that shit. I mean, I'm glad I can satisfy someone's sexual fantasy, but that definitely wasn't my intention.

Anyway, I really appreciate you a whole lot. I hope to get to know you even better from here on out! Seriously. Don't be afraid to contact me at the below information. xo.

Sincerely,
Austin James Robinson

KATE BELL,

If you're reading this, it's because you 'liked' or 'reacted' to a Facebook status I made back in April. I know, it's been awhile and I suck! I expect you to expect me to send you the Cheesecake Factory Menu or something – and honestly I will do that at a later time if you wish, – but this is a letter containing things I appreciate about you.

1). EVERYTHING. Wtf okay yeah I can't just write a 250-word paper on what I like about you. It could literally turn into a 250-page BOOK. Or 250 books, honestly. Remember that time I said I was going to eat 3,000 chicken nuggets by turning my mouth into a vacuum? That's just an aside. Anyway, literally wtf is our friendship? Like, actually. What if we actually become US Pres & VP in 2040? How fucked would the country be? VERY. I'm ready. #GiveUsMoney

2). Your ability to make everyone laugh and vote at the same time??? How the hell do you accomplish being the funniest and the most civically engaged person in everyone's life? What a concept, what a TALENT. I'm pretty sure everyone can attest to you being the sole important person in their life. That's why I have a shirt with your name on it. I'm prematurely capitalizing on your fame. I'm getting ready.

3). Your way of making friends with literally anyone and everyone. You literally don't judge or exclude anyone from your life – which is, like, probably the most iconic thing about you. Queen of being everyone's cup of tea. This, along with the previous points, definitely creates a formula to a little something called: YOU'RE GOING TO TAKE OVER THE WORLD. I won't be ready, but who will be?

Anyway, I really appreciate you a whole lot. I hope to get to know you even better from here on out! Seriously. Don't be afraid to contact me at the below information. xo.

Sincerely,
Austin James Robinson

[NAME REDACTED],

If you're reading this, it's because you 'liked' or 'reacted' to a Facebook status I made back in April. I know, it's been awhile and I suck! I expect you to expect me to send you the Cheesecake Factory Menu or something – and honestly I will do that at a later time if you wish, – but this is a letter containing things I appreciate about you.

1). Okay, so I'll admit: there's only so much I can say about you considering we've never really interacted with each other. Although I do remember the few times I've seen you or was in your presence, you were pretty f*cking hilarious. Also, it totally looked like you're reading to a bunch of [REDACTED] in your [REDACTED]. Like, you go out to the [REDACTED] and just pull out a book with the specific intention of reading to [REDACTED]. And I hope that's true. Also, I'm glad you're an [REDACTED] – for some reason I could totally see you [REDACTED] someday. Anyway! Here's a dumb story for you:

2). When I was in Kindergarten, I pooped my pants one day. I thought the logical thing to do would be to put the piece of poop inside another student's cubby. So, yeah, I did that. And it's all been downhill since then! ☺

Anyway, I really appreciate you a whole lot. I hope to get to know you even better from here on out! Seriously. Don't be afraid to contact me at the below information. xo.

Sincerely,
Austin James Robinson

[NAME REDACTED],

If you're reading this, it's because you 'liked' or 'reacted' to a Facebook status I made back in April. I know, it's been awhile and I suck! I expect you to expect me to send you the Cheesecake Factory Menu or something – and honestly I will do that at a later time if you wish, – but this is a letter containing things I appreciate about you.

1). How we were both integral to starting [REDACTED]. I know we really don't know each other much, but we both helped make [REDACTED] a reality, so that's pretty cool! But other than that, I can't really say much about you, and I don't want to bullshit this letter. So, do you want to hear a story about how I saw a professor snort cocaine instead?

2). Okay, so I went to the club once (it was, like, 6pm and I have no clue why I was there). This professor kept trying to buy me alcohol, but I don't really drink alcohol. So I just kept telling him that. Then he just kept making sexual advances toward me. But this was back when I was all "I'm abstinent – wahhh!" So, he couldn't help me there either! I tried to get him away from me by asking him if he had any cocaine, because I thought that might scare him off. Guess I know nothing about club culture! Because he sure did have some cocaine. Trying to call his bluff, I told him to whip it out and snort it. Anyway, you can guess how that night ended. With a lot of lessons learned!

Anyway, I really appreciate you a whole lot. I hope to get to know you even better from here on out! Seriously. Don't be afraid to contact me at the below information. xo.

Sincerely,
Austin James Robinson

PROJECT LETTERS

Katy Matz,

If you're reading this, it's because you 'liked' or 'reacted' to a Facebook status I made back in April. I know, it's been awhile and I suck! I expect you to expect me to send you the Cheesecake Factory Menu or something – and honestly I will do that at a later time if you wish, – but this is a letter containing things I appreciate about you.

1). How much freaking fun we had while on Study Abroad in England. You were one crazy girl, and I loved that so much. Remember that time we played some weird drinking game on the roof of your dorm? And we all, like, revealed secrets? What a time. And then that time we took a photo together where we were both dressed up as, like, 1700s women and I had a corset on my HEAD. We need to travel Europe together someday so we can just do those things again.

2). How dedicated you are to everything I do. From owning my AJR t-shirt to supporting me when I'm (for some reason) running for Student Government Vice President to signing up for my newsletter and reading every issue, you have always been there to support me. And I cannot thank you enough for doing all of that. Let me know if you EVER need support for ANYTHING, and I will certainly be there.

Anyway, I really appreciate you a whole lot. I hope to get to know you even better from here on out! Seriously. Don't be afraid to contact me at the below information. xo.

Sincerely,
Austin James Robinson

KC Poland,

If you're reading this, it's because you 'liked' or 'reacted' to a Facebook status I made back in April. I know, it's been awhile and I suck! I expect you to expect me to send you the Cheesecake Factory Menu or something – and honestly I will do that at a later time if you wish, – but this is a letter containing things I appreciate about you.

1). Sitting in front (or behind – honestly, who can never remember) of you in Chemistry class back in Sophomore year of high school. Wait, I just remembered that I also sat next to you in Freshman English class. Okay, cool, I have more content to go off of. I remember you always saying "DINNER" in English class. And, for some reason, I thought that was the funniest thing I had ever heard in my entire life (and it still is). And then you were just the funniest and smartest person in our Chemistry class. I remember you telling me about how you didn't do homework because you already knew all of the content. I thought that was the most iconic thing I ever heard in high school.

2). The time you told me about my boyfriend [REDACTED] messaging you about sending nudes to him, and then immediately helped me spread the rumor that he leaked poop because he had a gastrointestinal disease and had to wear a diaper. Also, gay people can teleport.

Anyway, I really appreciate you a whole lot. I hope to get to know you even better from here on out! Seriously. Don't be afraid to contact me at the below information. xo.

Sincerely,
Austin James Robinson

[NAME REDACTED],

If you're reading this, it's because you 'liked' or 'reacted' to a Facebook status I made back in April. I know, it's been awhile and I suck! I expect you to expect me to send you the Cheesecake Factory Menu or something – and honestly I will do that at a later time if you wish, – but this is a letter containing things I appreciate about you.

1). Your style / sense of fashion. I've always loved how you looked during our [REDACTED] courses / while in [REDACTED]. Kind of like dark beauty. I cannot even describe it, but I have definitely never met anyone else with your specific style. You should be a model! If you want, of course. (But definitely do it.)

2). How open to learning and service you are. I see this through both [REDACTED] and [REDACTED] (I guess the only two communities we were both apart of, so it makes sense): you are always asking questions and willing to be the one to help, even if you appear shy at first. You have nothing but kindness and good in your heart, and that's apparent when anyone gets to know you.

3). The fact that you've supported me through my many weird projects! First: you own an AUSTIN JAMES ROBINSON t-shirt. Amazing. Those were so fun, until they made me believe I could definitely run for Student Government Vice President. And then you totally asked for a profile picture! I'm so lucky to have people like you in my life, even if I may not always show it.

Anyway, I really appreciate you a whole lot. I hope to get to know you even better from here on out! Seriously. Don't be afraid to contact me at the below information. xo.

Sincerely,
Austin James Robinson

[NAME REDACTED],

If you're reading this, it's because you 'liked' or 'reacted' to a Facebook status I made back in April. I know, it's been awhile and I suck! I expect you to expect me to send you the Cheesecake Factory Menu or something – and honestly I will do that at a later time if you wish, – but this is a letter containing things I appreciate about you.

1). The fact that we worked at a [REDACTED] together. I think that was literally the only time we ever saw each other in person. And I know we didn't talk much because I was only there for a short amount of time every day for about a month or so. But it was still pretty cool to get to work with you.

2). How you and [REDACTED] are funny af. I really appreciate y'all's sense of humor. Y'all don't take anything too seriously, and you're willing to make fun of whatever. Iconic.

3). Wanna hear a story about how I stole [REDACTED] from the place we worked at? Okay, that sounds way worse than it actually is. You know how they owned a machine that would count the [REDACTED], and then we would have to recount the [REDACTED] manually? And if the machine [REDACTED], we'd legally have to throw away [REDACTED]? What a waste! One time one of the [REDACTED], so I [REDACTED]. I ended up throwing them in a dumpster later on, but I thought it would be funny to [REDACTED]. Then I realized it would actually be really, really stupid. So, anyway.

Anyway, I really appreciate you a whole lot. I hope to get to know you even better from here on out! Seriously. Don't be afraid to contact me at the below information. xo.

Sincerely,
Austin James Robinson

[NAME REDACTED],

If you're reading this, it's because you 'liked' or 'reacted' to a Facebook status I made back in April. I know, it's been awhile and I suck! I expect you to expect me to send you the Cheesecake Factory Menu or something – and honestly I will do that at a later time if you wish, – but this is a letter containing things I appreciate about you.

1). How we initially met literally an hour before I was supposed to hear about whether or not I won Student Body Vice President (or rather, when they delayed the results for a month). Remember that? We ate at [REDACTED] and we talked about [REDACTED] ([REDACTED], if you're reading this, we talked shit) and [REDACTED] ([REDACTED], if you're reading this, it was all praise). What a time.

2). Your sense of humor. You always send me naughty emoji chain texts and memes, and that's what I've always loved about you. Plus, you watch all of the shows I tell you to watch. And you're genuinely a good friend and cool.

3). That weird time in our lives in which we sort of had a [REDACTED] to an extent, but really what??? We, like, hung out and [REDACTED] for a hot week or two because I think we were [REDACTED]? Or maybe we just [REDACTED]. Who can never ben sure? And remember when we planned that road trip to [REDACTED]? But never went? Amazing.

Anyway, I really appreciate you a whole lot. I hope to get to know you even better from here on out! Seriously. Don't be afraid to contact me at the below information. xo.

Sincerely,
Austin James Robinson

Kizer Shelton,

If you're reading this, it's because you 'liked' or 'reacted' to a Facebook status I made back in April. I know, it's been awhile and I suck! I expect you to expect me to send you the Cheesecake Factory Menu or something – and honestly I will do that at a later time if you wish, – but this is a letter containing things I appreciate about you.

1). How you, you are. You're so fucking original and creative. I LOVE it. Plus, you don't give a shit about what anyone thinks about how you conduct your life or what their opinion might be of you. You are perfectly living your reality, and there's no shame whatsoever in it. It's very inspiring. Keep doing it because surely you are giving hope to tons of people who need to see people being themselves so that they may one day have the courage to do the same.

2). How you're in school for writing and graphic design! Those two subjects are literally my loves. I'm very fortunate enough to be able to write and have a degree in it, but what I would give to know how to be good at graphic design! I'm so excited for you to finish your degree and have all these awesome skills in the arts. I cannot wait to see what you produce later on!

Anyway, I really appreciate you a whole lot. I hope to get to know you even better from here on out! Seriously. Don't be afraid to contact me at the below information. xo.

Sincerely,
Austin James Robinson

PROJECT LETTERS

Kori Morris,

If you're reading this, it's because you 'liked' or 'reacted' to a Facebook status I made back in April. I know, it's been awhile and I suck! I expect you to expect me to send you the Cheesecake Factory Menu or something – and honestly I will do that at a later time if you wish, – but this is a letter containing things I appreciate about you.

1). Your willingness to open up dialogue and discuss difficult topics. Okay, so this might apply to most of us within the Rapoport Scholarship community, but I remember you being one of the most willing and eager participants to discuss the topics in our courses with Eric Bowles. It was amazing, and I'm really glad people like you exist at UT, and on this world in general, so we can always be thinking critically about issues facing the world today. I know it can be exhausting, but it's great work and I'm incredibly glad I was able to experience the class's discussions with you involved. (Also, you always ask questions and that goes hand-in-hand with this point.)

2). The way you conduct yourself in regard to service and helping the world. Again, not uncommon in our scholarship group, but you excel in this area. You take the phrase "What Starts Here Changes The World" and exemplify it. You are always willing to volunteer or help out a service-related group on our campus, and it becomes infectious. I can't wait to see where you end up in this world.

Anyway, I really appreciate you a whole lot. I hope to get to know you even better from here on out! Seriously. Don't be afraid to contact me at the below information. xo.

Sincerely,
Austin James Robinson

[NAME REDACTED],

If you're reading this, it's because you 'liked' or 'reacted' to a Facebook status I made back in April. I know, it's been awhile and I suck! I expect you to expect me to send you the Cheesecake Factory Menu or something – and honestly I will do that at a later time if you wish, – but this is a letter containing things I appreciate about you.

1). The fact that we're from different generations, but that we are still brothers in Alpha Phi Omega. I love how APO does that to people – I could meet someone ENTIRELY different from me, and we'd still have that connection. I love that. It's so nice to know an older brother. However, as you know, we don't really know anything about each other! And I want to change that. But for now, I'm not going to pretend like I know you. So here's a story about me!

2). When I was in Los Angeles last summer, I was super sad for some reason and decided to walk for two hours in no known direction. I got on some dating apps because that's clearly logical to do when you're sad, and this guy kept telling me that he wanted to meet me. I told him I was too sad to talk, so he told me he just wanted to wave at me from his car. That sounded pretty funny, so I agreed. However, when he passed by me, he completely stopped! Dick! That wasn't our deal! Anyway, he was driving a convertible white Jaguar, so of course I got in (I was too sad to care that this was a stranger). I ended up finding out that he used to be a wildly successful chiropractor in LA until he decided to leave the business to become a spiritual healer for pets! He even has his own Wikipedia page! Anyway, that was fun.

Anyway, I really appreciate you a whole lot. I hope to get to know you even better from here on out! Seriously. Don't be afraid to contact me at the below information. xo.

Sincerely,
Austin James Robinson

Kourtney Elaine,

If you're reading this, it's because you 'liked' or 'reacted' to a Facebook status I made back in April. I know, it's been awhile and I suck! I expect you to expect me to send you the Cheesecake Factory Menu or something – and honestly I will do that at a later time if you wish, – but this is a letter containing things I appreciate about you.

1). How we were both in the Health Science track in high school together. I remember you sat right in front of me for the nursing practicum class. You were, like, one of the smartest and hardest working students in the class! I hope you ended up being able to use your CNA skills in the real world! Remember when we took that mirror picture together (with [REDACTED], as well) in the nursing home? Iconic.

2). How big your goals are! We had a conversation recently, and you are DEFINITELY thinking about health science in your life goals! That's more than I can say for myself. That's so awesome. I hope you finish up your degree in General Psychology and then go on to be an amazing Psychiatrist! Let me know how your aspirations work out!

Anyway, I really appreciate you a whole lot. I hope to get to know you even better from here on out! Seriously. Don't be afraid to contact me at the below information. xo.

Sincerely,
Austin James Robinson

Kyle Garza,

If you're reading this, it's because you 'liked' or 'reacted' to a Facebook status I made back in April. I know, it's been awhile and I suck! I expect you to expect me to send you the Cheesecake Factory Menu or something – and honestly I will do that at a later time if you wish, – but this is a letter containing things I appreciate about you.

1). The fact that we were both in Alpha Phi Omega. That's just really cool to me. We're technically #Brothers. Do you feel like my brother? Would you feel comfortable calling me that if we ever saw each other in public?

2). How you're in the Longhorn Band. Is that what it's called? Like, I freaking love people in band, but I honestly have no clue what our band is called because I just don't go to sports games. But I do really enjoy that you're in the band. I wish I knew what music was so I could be in band!

3). So this doesn't really have to do with you (I'm running out of things to say), but one time I went to Walmart and the elderly guy who was the greeter told me that he created the sticky part of diapers. You know those side things on the diaper that you peel and then pull over the other part of the diaper once the baby is in it? He told me that he created that. I was, like, five-years-old at the time.

Anyway, I really appreciate you a whole lot. I hope to get to know you even better from here on out! Seriously. Don't be afraid to contact me at the below information. xo.

Sincerely,
Austin James Robinson

EDIT: I did not meet him in APO – he's just closely affiliated with APO.

Kyle Kirby,

If you're reading this, it's because you 'liked' or 'reacted' to a Facebook status I made back in April. I know, it's been awhile and I suck! I expect you to expect me to send you the Cheesecake Factory Menu or something – and honestly I will do that at a later time if you wish, – but this is a letter containing things I appreciate about you.

1). The fact that you live super close to my mother's hometown of Saint John, New Brunswick, Canada. I know we matched on a dating app while I was spending some time there, so I'm still surprised that we're friends on Facebook! Regardless, I love having friends from that part of the world. Thanks for not deleting me!

2). Speaking on that dating app (am I allowed to say the name of it, or will I get sued?), here's a list of pretty good prospective biographies for you to use if you want:
- "In prison. If you want to meet me, you have to give them my ID number. It's #002481. Don't tell them that I have a phone in here – just say you're my brother or something."
- "Check out my website! www.pornhub.com"
- "Looking for a drinking partner! And my parents! Where are my parents ☹"
- "In a committed relationship with GOD. We decided we're gonna try an open relationship."

Anyway, I really appreciate you a whole lot. I hope to get to know you even better from here on out! Seriously. Don't be afraid to contact me at the below information. xo.

Sincerely,
Austin James Robinson

UPDATE: He actually used one of the bios.

Kyra Glenn,

If you're reading this, it's because you 'liked' or 'reacted' to a Facebook status I made back in April. I know, it's been awhile and I suck! I expect you to expect me to send you the Cheesecake Factory Menu or something – and honestly I will do that at a later time if you wish, – but this is a letter containing things I appreciate about you.

1). How we used to make fun of people who supported KONY 2012 back in high school. You were the ONLY other person in the entire school who understood that that campaign was a complete scam. It's so funny to have just one other person beside you as you look at other people and say, "Wtf – are you really THAT stupid?" And then we could laugh together when the CEO, like, masturbated in public while under the influence – and the believers just ignored it. What a TIME.

2). The fact that you're now basically the face of my brand. LOL. How did this even happen? I'm so glad you're doing modeling and that you've found someone like Rob who can be a creative power partner with you! Y'all are literally going to take over the photography / modeling realm together. I can't wait for that.

3). Your sense of humor. You aren't afraid to laugh at anything and everything, and you don't take yourself too seriously (in a good way). So glad to have someone like you in my life who can just LAUGH.

Anyway, I really appreciate you a whole lot. I hope to get to know you even better from here on out! Seriously. Don't be afraid to contact me at the below information. xo.

Sincerely,
Austin James Robinson

Lauren Balentine,

If you're reading this, it's because you 'liked' or 'reacted' to a Facebook status I made back in April. I know, it's been awhile and I suck! I expect you to expect me to send you the Cheesecake Factory Menu or something – and honestly I will do that at a later time if you wish, – but this is a letter containing things I appreciate about you.

1). Our time together during our Study Abroad summer at the University of Oxford. I know we didn't hang out – like, I actually think we didn't hang out once. Hell, we probably said, like, five words to each other the entire time. We were definitely in extremely different friend groups there. But I do remember you being pretty funny. And I wish I would have gotten to know you while I was there! Regardless, we have the fact that we spent a summer in Europe in common, and that's pretty cool.

2). Although we were in different friend groups at Oxford, when we got back to the university, it was surprising to see how many mutual friends we have! Also, how f*cking hilarious you are online. I definitely got to know you so much better through your posts – they also made me appreciate you so much. Continue being who you are, because you're amazing!

Anyway, I really appreciate you a whole lot. I hope to get to know you even better from here on out! Seriously. Don't be afraid to contact me at the below information. xo.

Sincerely,
Austin James Robinson

[NAME REDACTED],

If you're reading this, it's because you 'liked' or 'reacted' to a Facebook status I made back in April. I know, it's been awhile and I suck! I expect you to expect me to send you the Cheesecake Factory Menu or something – and honestly I will do that at a later time if you wish, – but this is a letter containing things I appreciate about you.

1). How dedicated you were to [REDACTED]. I know we didn't know each other that well considering I think you were graduating while I was coming into university. BUT I remember getting to know you very well over the several [REDACTED] seminars and things that we both attended. I believe you were an [REDACTED], and that's amazing to me! I always had the hopes and dreams to make it onto [REDACTED], so you were certainly a hero in my eyes. I wish we could have been in [REDACTED] together a little longer, but I'm glad I got to meet you and hang out with you in [REDACTED] regardless!

2). The fact that you're a [REDACTED]! Talk about giving yourself to others outside of your [REDACTED] life! You're the type of person we need more of in this world: constantly serving and giving themselves to others in every realm of your life!

Anyway, I really appreciate you a whole lot. I hope to get to know you even better from here on out! Seriously. Don't be afraid to contact me at the below information. xo.

Sincerely,
Austin James Robinson

PROJECT LETTERS

Leslie Solcher,

If you're reading this, it's because you 'liked' or 'reacted' to a Facebook status I made back in April. I know, it's been awhile and I suck! I expect you to expect me to send you the Cheesecake Factory Menu or something – and honestly I will do that at a later time if you wish, – but this is a letter containing things I appreciate about you.

1). That time that you inspired me to live-tweet you the entirety of the first episode of that terrible show. What was it called again? Oh yeah – actually, no, I literally forgot what it was called. I was gonna make some big entrance with the title in all caps, but I literally can't care less to even Google the show. I think it had Drew Barrymore in it? And it was about her eating other human beings? Quirky af, am I right? Anyway, you're welcome (and thank you).

2). How we talked every day for, like, not even a month and now we don't talk anymore. To be fair, we're both pretty wild. Like, literally. I doubt we could even handle each other in person. We should try it sometime, but I wouldn't mind if we didn't because I'm not looking to DIE anytime soon.

3). Our mutual connection to [REDACTED]. This is a whole point because we need to pay respect to the fact that [REDACTED] has graced our lives. I cry sometimes thinking about how there's so many people in the world, and so many places, and somehow we ended up in this one with [REDACTED] in our life (crying emoji).

Anyway, I really appreciate you a whole lot. I hope to get to know you even better from here on out! Seriously. Don't be afraid to contact me at the below information. xo.

Sincerely,
Austin James Robinson

Livie Venegas,

If you're reading this, it's because you 'liked' or 'reacted' to a Facebook status I made back in April. I know, it's been awhile and I suck! I expect you to expect me to send you the Cheesecake Factory Menu or something – and honestly I will do that at a later time if you wish, – but this is a letter containing things I appreciate about you.

1). How you, you are. You are yourself, and you are unapologetic about that. I love that. It takes a lot of courage to come out in any form and fashion, and you know you have a great support network. I hope I'm apart of that. I hope you continue to be yourself and love yourself and do everything you want to do from here on out!

2). How we played Rock Band that one time and I really sucked at it! Yeah, I'm really bad at that game. But even though I'm bad, it was really fun to play with you, and I hope we can do that again sometime!

3). The fact that you know who Alan Resnick is! Okay, so, like, no one in my life even knows who he is, so it's so amazing to find someone who actually knows who he is and likes his content. Let's have an Alan Resnick party sometime.

4). A fourth thing! Let's make a fourth thing to be appreciative about in the future!

Anyway, I really appreciate you a whole lot. I hope to get to know you even better from here on out! Seriously. Don't be afraid to contact me at the below information. xo.

Sincerely,
Austin James Robinson

Madison Harwell,

If you're reading this, it's because you 'liked' or 'reacted' to a Facebook status I made back in April. I know, it's been awhile and I suck! I expect you to expect me to send you the Cheesecake Factory Menu or something – and honestly I will do that at a later time if you wish, – but this is a letter containing things I appreciate about you.

1). Okay, so this is embarrassing, but I feel like we totally don't know each other that well at all. Definitely not enough to warrant a whole page, which is definitely my fault as a friend. However, I'll write you a story, instead:

2). So, this one time my friend was all, "I'm apart of this gym! If you sign up, it'll only be $100 because I'll refer you!" And I was like, "I don't know what a gym is or what muscles are, but sure!" Anyway, so I totally paid the $100 upfront and I was able to go to the gym – **WHICH WAS LOCATED RIGHT NEXT TO MY APARTMENT** – any day at any time forever and ever for 365 days. Every day if I wanted! But you know what I apparently wanted instead?? To not go one **SINGLE TIME**. Literally, never to even step food near it for a full year. I basically donated to that gym. As if I'm just so into the process of gyms, but I just don't like working out myself.

3). I don't know why I'm numbering this, but now that I'm thinking about it, that was more of a life lesson than a story. Advice to you: don't buy a full year gym membership if you don't know what you're even doing in life

Anyway, I really appreciate you a whole lot. I hope to get to know you even better from here on out! Seriously. Don't be afraid to contact me at the below information. xo.

Sincerely,
Austin James Robinson

UPDATE: Apparently she has actually done the SAME exact thing. Double lesson learned.

[NAME REDACTED],

If you're reading this, it's because you 'liked' or 'reacted' to a Facebook status I made back in April. I know, it's been awhile and I suck! I expect you to expect me to send you the Cheesecake Factory Menu or something – and honestly I will do that at a later time if you wish, – but this is a letter containing things I appreciate about you.

1). How dedicated you are to [REDACTED]. When I think about [REDACTED] or hear about it, you almost always come to mind; and we barely even talk or know each other that well! Well, I guess now you're past your [REDACTED]. Unless you [REDACTED] again??? Honestly, I graduated back in December, so I have NO CLUE who the [REDACTED] even is. Oops. Also, I don't know you that well, so here's a story about my sister-goat:

2). So when I was, like, 6-years-old, my grandparents found a dying baby goat (a KID) on the side of the road. They took her home and put a diaper on her and started bottle-feeding her and treating her like a dog. Like, legitimately, this goat was domesticated af. And she grew up right beside me. She was kind of like the sister I never had. Except she was a goat. Anyway! I hope you enjoyed that story!

Anyway, I really appreciate you a whole lot. I hope to get to know you even better from here on out! Seriously. Don't be afraid to contact me at the below information. xo.

Sincerely,
Austin James Robinson

PROJECT LETTERS

Mark Witte,

If you're reading this, it's because you 'liked' or 'reacted' to a Facebook status I made back in April. I know, it's been awhile and I suck! I expect you to expect me to send you the Cheesecake Factory Menu or something – and honestly I will do that at a later time if you wish, – but this is a letter containing things I appreciate about you.

1). The fact that your sister created the design for the Tide Pod, which influenced, like, every other company's wash pods and, thus, changed the face of washing clothes. Iconic. When you first told me that, I… I lost it. I started buying all of the Tide Pods at Target. I couldn't get enough. I was using them for every single piece of clothing. One Tide Pod to one piece of clothing. I told everyone about them. Your sister changed my life.

2). When you took me to Half Priced Books and pretended to be my father, even though you're literally, like, 4 years younger than me. And honestly, if I wouldn't have started laughing, you MAY have been able to pull it off. I look forward to bamboozling more and more people with you.

3). How we're inappropriately in love but we show it through joking about how we'll never be together. But we both know who our true love is: Austin Smith.

Anyway, I really appreciate you a whole lot. I hope to get to know you even better from here on out! Seriously. Don't be afraid to contact me at the below information. xo.

Sincerely,
Austin James Robinson

Marshall Geyer,

If you're reading this, it's because you 'liked' or 'reacted' to a Facebook status I made back in April. I know, it's been awhile and I suck! I expect you to expect me to send you the Cheesecake Factory Menu or something – and honestly I will do that at a later time if you wish, – but this is a letter containing things I appreciate about you.

1). Being online friends with you for the longest time before I ever met you. I thought you were the funniest person, and I really enjoyed the illusion of not truly knowing who you were. Then I saw you as you were walking away from Round Up and I was (for some reason) going to Round Up, and I was like, "Are you Marshall Geyer???" and then it was pretty fun. And since then I think I've seen you, like, one and a half times.

2). Going to that comedy show and you constantly just joking about how the comedian had no legs because he was wearing camouflage pants. I'm pretty sure we didn't listen to a single joke the comedian was saying because you were too busy laughing your ass off about that fact. You kept telling me to scream, "WHERE ARE YOUR LEGS?" and I refused. I think you actually ended up screaming it that night. You wild.

3). Your cousin, who always likes my stuff but never adds me as a friend on Facebook. I love her. She's my biggest fan. Thank you.

Anyway, I really appreciate you a whole lot. I hope to get to know you even better from here on out! Seriously. Don't be afraid to contact me at the below information. xo.

Sincerely,
Austin James Robinson

[NAME REDACTED],

If you're reading this, it's because you 'liked' or 'reacted' to a Facebook status I made back in April. I know, it's been awhile and I suck! I expect you to expect me to send you the Cheesecake Factory Menu or something – and honestly I will do that at a later time if you wish, – but this is a letter containing things I appreciate about you.

1). How incredibly smart you are. I mean, [REDACTED]?? You're literally the only person I know who goes there. In fact, I think you're the only person I know who's even smart enough to go there. Not saying that [REDACTED] and smartness go hand-in-hand, but still: damn. I remember when I was talking with you and [REDACTED] about university during a [REDACTED] meet and you told me you were going to [REDACTED] – I was happy simply for the fact that I come from a town where no one even really goes to [REDACTED]. Anyway, I hope you've had the time of your life there. I'm not sure if you're still there or if you've [REDACTED] and now you're immediately the next ruler of the universe. Wouldn't be surprised.

2). That time we snail-mailed each other, like, once and that was that. I have no clue how that started or ended, but do you remember that? I just remember freaking out because someone from [REDACTED] was mailing me. I was so DUMB back then – I have no clue why I placed so much importance in the simple fact that you go / went to [REDACTED]. I probably annoyed the hell out of you.

Anyway, I really appreciate you a whole lot. I hope to get to know you even better from here on out! Seriously. Don't be afraid to contact me at the below information. xo.

Sincerely,
Austin James Robinson

Mary Kvinta,

If you're reading this, it's because you 'liked' or 'reacted' to a Facebook status I made back in April. I know, it's been awhile and I suck! I expect you to expect me to send you the Cheesecake Factory Menu or something – and honestly I will do that at a later time if you wish, – but this is a letter containing things I appreciate about you.

1). All of the Study Abroad / Oxford memories that we have together. That was such a fun time and I wish we could do it all over again (cry face emoji). Remember when we went to a castle in, like, Wales (I think) and I went into the "DANGER: KEEP OUT" zone because I'm punk af? Or when we got my face painted in Port Smith (honestly, I keep forgetting what some of those places are called, so sorry if I butcher them all). Anyway, thanks for all of the UK memories!!!

2). The fact that you're in Plan II. That's, like, my absolute favorite academic program at the University of Texas. Even though I make fun of it literally 100% of the time. I was actually DENIED (rude!) when I applied to it, so I get to live vicariously through you now!

Anyway, I really appreciate you a whole lot. I hope to get to know you even better from here on out! Seriously. Don't be afraid to contact me at the below information. xo.

Sincerely,
Austin James Robinson

Matthew McKellar,

If you're reading this, it's because you 'liked' or 'reacted' to a Facebook status I made back in April. I know, it's been awhile and I suck! I expect you to expect me to send you the Cheesecake Factory Menu or something – and honestly I will do that at a later time if you wish, – but this is a letter containing things I appreciate about you.

1). How nice you are. Like, definitely the "nice guy" stereotype (not saying you're a stereotype – just that you're extremely nice, and I really appreciate that about you). Did this even sound like a compliment? I guess I'm terrible at those. Regardless, this is DEFINITELY a good thing! Every single time we ever hung out, you were the sweetest person ever. Thank you for that.

2). How we both saw Christina Grimmie perform live about half a year before she died. I honestly had no clue who she was before going to the concert – so it was pretty surreal to see her in the news. It was a fun concert! I remember forcing her to sign my neck.

3). How cool you are even though I was a dick to you. I definitely led you on and made you think something more was going to happen between us. And I'm glad you told me sternly about how you felt, but that you're also still in my life. I'm really sorry for how I treated you. I was in a terrible place, but that's no excuse.

Anyway, I really appreciate you a whole lot. I hope to get to know you even better from here on out! Seriously. Don't be afraid to contact me at the below information. xo.

Sincerely,
Austin James Robinson

Matthew Shin,

If you're reading this, it's because you 'liked' or 'reacted' to a Facebook status I made back in April. I know, it's been awhile and I suck! I expect you to expect me to send you the Cheesecake Factory Menu or something – and honestly I will do that at a later time if you wish, – but this is a letter containing things I appreciate about you.

1). The simple fact that you're a Computer Science major. Did you know that CS is my all-time favorite major at the University of Texas, and also my favorite thing in the world? I have a ton of CS friends because I won't stay away from y'all's building at the uni. I legitimately tried to join LAN but they denied me because I was an English-Education major and, thus, nowhere near CS. Isn't that rude? Anyway, so I'm super happy you work in CS. Thanks. I can now continue my collection of CS friends.

2). Your support toward my brand and everything that I do with it. You've messaged me about it a couple of times, and you've even bought my book! I love when people take interest in what I do and aren't completely weirded out or intimidated by it (trust me, there's people like that). I hope to keep cranking out content to impress you <3

Anyway, I really appreciate you a whole lot. I hope to get to know you even better from here on out! Seriously. Don't be afraid to contact me at the below information. xo.

Sincerely,
Austin James Robinson

Max Dozier,

If you're reading this, it's because you 'liked' or 'reacted' to a Facebook status I made back in April. I know, it's been awhile and I suck! I expect you to expect me to send you the Cheesecake Factory Menu or something – and honestly I will do that at a later time if you wish, – but this is a letter containing things I appreciate about you.

1). The fact that when I first met you, I thought you were literally a substitute teacher, and then me, [REDACTED], and [REDACTED] all fell in love with you, and then you appropriately left all of us. What a ride that was. Luckily once you went back to Tucson, I was able to see you, like, 20thousand times. Which brings me to my next point…

2). The fact that I've been to Tucson, Arizona more than any other city in the United States due to the simple fact that you live there, and I get to see my #TucsonBoys. Remember when we pretended to make a boy band named after me and took pictures via iPhone at that rich-ass outlet mall? Amazing. Let's do more of that soon.

3). How I know, like, all of your family at this point. I mean, I'm sure there's an aunt and uncle or two (maybe a dog) that I haven't met yet, but I've still met a pretty good portion of them.

Anyway, I really appreciate you a whole lot. I hope to get to know you even better from here on out! Seriously. Don't be afraid to contact me at the below information. xo.

Sincerely,
Austin James Robinson

Max Healy,

If you're reading this, it's because you 'liked' or 'reacted' to a Facebook status I made back in April. I know, it's been awhile and I suck! I expect you to expect me to send you the Cheesecake Factory Menu or something – and honestly I will do that at a later time if you wish, – but this is a letter containing things I appreciate about you.

1). The fact that basically your first ever message to me was, "You're gay." And I had no clue who you were or why we were even friends on Facebook, but I appreciated that. You then followed up with, "Idiot." Iconic. The start of a friendship. I will never forget it.

2). Your writing. You've talked about writing a lot to me. You've discussed writing a book for November Novel Writing Month (or whatever – I really can't remember the exact title at this moment), and you've also talked with me about publishing a book. I think the majority of our conversations nowadays are about writing books, so I cannot wait to see where you go with writing. Keep doing it.

3). How insightful you are. You always talk about society and politics, and it always becomes apparent to me that you're much smarter than I am. Likewise, one time you told me about how you go to the local mental hospitals and talk with homeless people, and that's some pretty cool and nice shit.

Anyway, I really appreciate you a whole lot. I hope to get to know you even better from here on out! Seriously. Don't be afraid to contact me at the below information. xo.

Sincerely,
Austin James Robinson

PROJECT LETTERS

Max Ollig,

If you're reading this, it's because you 'liked' or 'reacted' to a Facebook status I made back in April. I know, it's been awhile and I suck! I expect you to expect me to send you the Cheesecake Factory Menu or something – and honestly I will do that at a later time if you wish, – but this is a letter containing things I appreciate about you.

1). Okay, so I'm going to admit that I absolutely do not know you that well (but you probably know that). I know that we went to the JSA Stanford Summer School together, but other than that, I cannot recall a single time we talked or discussed anything. I mean, you called me hilarious once via message – and that means a lot to me. Anyway, I guess I could just tell you a story instead:

2). Okay, so do you remember when Chick-Fil-A got #ExPoSeD for being, like, anti-gay or something? And then all of the gay people got pissed and decided that the logical thing to do was to kiss each other on a very specific day in front of every single Chick-Fil-A in the nation? Well, like, that not only created great marketing for Chick-Fil-A, for one, but also it created this weird love event where everyone was macking on each other at this fast food establishment. What I mean is: after the whole gay kissing happened, the STRAIGHT people then decided that they'd have their own day to kiss each other in front of Chick-Fil-As around the nation. What is up with people??? Regardless, what Chick-Fil-A's real crime is is the fact that they got, like, everyone in the entire USA to make out with each other in front of their restaurant. And since then, I've been eating there.

Anyway, I really appreciate you a whole lot. I hope to get to know you even better from here on out! Seriously. Don't be afraid to contact me at the below information. xo.

Sincerely,
Austin James Robinson

[NAME REDACTED],

If you're reading this, it's because you 'liked' or 'reacted' to a Facebook status I made back in April. I know, it's been awhile and I suck! I expect you to expect me to send you the Cheesecake Factory Menu or something – and honestly I will do that at a later time if you wish, – but this is a letter containing things I appreciate about you.

1). Hi! I don't think we've ever met before! So instead of writing a bunch of bullshit about what I like about you, here's a story about how I really love all-American restaurants and still buy their 2 for $20 even though I'm single:

2). Okay, so I promise that I used to have a boyfriend. And me and that guy would buy the 2 for $20 deals at popular American chain restaurants, such as Chili's and Applebee's. We would usually order to-go because I hate eating out and I love eating in! Anyway, I broke up with him. And you know what I did next? I continued to order the 2 for $20 deals all by myself! I would just spread all of the food across, like, four meals! It was really great and fiscally smart, basically! I mean, yeah, it was sort of sad considering the fact that I was ordering two full meals for myself, but honestly, yes.

Anyway, I really appreciate you a whole lot. I hope to get to know you even better from here on out! Seriously. Don't be afraid to contact me at the below information. xo.

Sincerely,
Austin James Robinson

PROJECT LETTERS

Megan Hahn,

If you're reading this, it's because you 'liked' or 'reacted' to a Facebook status I made back in April. I know, it's been awhile and I suck! I expect you to expect me to send you the Cheesecake Factory Menu or something – and honestly I will do that at a later time if you wish, – but this is a letter containing things I appreciate about you.

1). How I met you through another Student Government Executive Alliance campaign. I made a lot of friends through that, but you were one of the only people who I continued to talk to and became good friends with. I love how we were all expected to be pitted against each other, and somehow ended up making friends with tons of people from the other campaigns.

2). That time we went to the Cheesecake Factory and you got three gravy boats full of ranch. Remember that? Wasn't that totally embarrassing for you? You thought that they were gonna give you small cups of ranch and, instead, they brought out these huge gravy boats filled to the brim with ranch. And you didn't know what to do. Amazing.

3). Our mutual friend, who shall not be named. Well, who can never be sure whether or not we can consider him a friend anymore. This sounds like tea, but I just wanted to bring it up because we really bonded over the fact that he's been a dick to us over the past half a year. Oops, tea spilled.

Anyway, I really appreciate you a whole lot. I hope to get to know you even better from here on out! Seriously. Don't be afraid to contact me at the below information. xo.

Sincerely,
Austin James Robinson

[NAME REDACTED],

If you're reading this, it's because you 'liked' or 'reacted' to a Facebook status I made back in April. I know, it's been awhile and I suck! I expect you to expect me to send you the Cheesecake Factory Menu or something – and honestly I will do that at a later time if you wish, – but this is a letter containing things I appreciate about you.

1). Okay, so awk: I totally don't really know you that well AT ALL. Definitely not well enough to warrant me writing a 250-word letter to you (which is EMBARRASSING on my part). But regardless, here's a story:

2). Okay so, like, I REALLY love French fries, right? I was a vegetarian for 2.5 years and basically I was really dumb and only ate French fries all of the time. I would literally go up to McDonald's or Wendy's and ask them for French fries and SOME BUNS so I could make a French fry sandwich. They hated me. Anyway, one time I was going through the Popeye's drive-thru and I really wanted to just shove some French fries down my throat – that was IN at the time for me. I told them I would like the FAMILY-SIZE French fry. They literally responded, "Sir, that feeds four people." You know what I said? "I want two, then." Kidding, that is not what happened. I just said, "Yes" like a good boy and let them SHAME me. And the French fries aren't even good there.

Anyway, I really appreciate you a whole lot. I hope to get to know you even better from here on out! Seriously. Don't be afraid to contact me at the below information. xo.

Sincerely,
Austin James Robinson

[NAME REDACTED],

If you're reading this, it's because you 'liked' or 'reacted' to a Facebook status I made back in April. I know, it's been awhile and I suck! I expect you to expect me to send you the Cheesecake Factory Menu or something – and honestly I will do that at a later time if you wish, – but this is a letter containing things I appreciate about you.

1). Your hair. Never cut it. Literally keep growing it out. Let it consume you. Become hair. I used to really want to reach your level of hair expertise, but then I chopped all of my hair off and I don't think I'm ever going back. I'm giving up. I'm sorry.

2). Your dedication to the Dror/Shannon campaign. When I think of that campaign, I pretty much think of Jonathan, Delisa, and you. That was a pretty sick time. And I can't believe we became friends because of it! It's also always pretty cool when a student is civically engaged on any level of politics – and Student Government is pretty cool, I guess.

3). You're Jewish. I know you can't control that, so idk if this is a shitty thing for me to say I like about you. BUT, I guess what I mean is that I had never met a Jewish person before going to university – I come from a town in the middle of nowhere. And I've been looking into converting to Judaism for two years now. It's a pretty serious thing and so I kind of enjoy having Jewish friends to discuss it with. I know we haven't necessarily talked about it at all, but maybe soon. (Jewish or not, you also have a pretty kick-ass personality and I know tons of people love you.)

Anyway, I really appreciate you a whole lot. I hope to get to know you even better from here on out! Seriously. Don't be afraid to contact me at the below information. xo.

Sincerely,
Austin James Robinson

Mohammad Syed,

If you're reading this, it's because you 'liked' or 'reacted' to a Facebook status I made back in April. I know, it's been awhile and I suck! I expect you to expect me to send you the Cheesecake Factory Menu or something – and honestly I will do that at a later time if you wish, – but this is a letter containing things I appreciate about you.

1). The simple fact that you're in Texas Blazers. I know this is a silly reason to appreciate you, but honestly: we have not really talked much and I don't know much about you (my fault). But the fact that you're in the same organization as me (especially Texas Blazers) means a lot and tells me that we have a lot more in common than we think we do. I hope to get to know you better in the future.

2). I'M PRETTY SURE YOU KIND OF SECRETLY INTRODUCED ME TO 21 SAVAGE. Okay, so when I was on selection committee for your new guy semester, I came across an application (blind) in which the person discussed their newest favorite rapper being 21 Savage. Now, I love rap, like, way too much. So I decided to look him up and give him a listen. That is ALL I listened to for the rest of my days on Selection Committee (you can ask the other guys). And it sucked because I literally could not thank the individual who technically showed me this amazing rapper. Anyway, I'm pretty sure that person was you considering you talk about him a lot. SO I'M GLAD YOU GOT INTO TEXAS BLAZERS.

Anyway, I really appreciate you a whole lot. I hope to get to know you even better from here on out! Seriously. Don't be afraid to contact me at the below information. xo.

Sincerely,
Austin James Robinson

PROJECT LETTERS

Molly Walsh,

If you're reading this, it's because you 'liked' or 'reacted' to a Facebook status I made back in April. I know, it's been awhile and I suck! I expect you to expect me to send you the Cheesecake Factory Menu or something – and honestly I will do that at a later time if you wish, – but this is a letter containing things I appreciate about you.

1). The fact that we met at HOBY and still talk to each other. I mean, I talk to some other people that I met at HOBY, but not many. And I know we're from the same HOBY, so it's even less of a miracle, BUT STILL. I love how your ENTIRE family continually comes back to HOBY. Amazing. Y'all are so dedicated to the point where y'all basically run the entire thing. What are we going to do when y'all are gone? The entirety of HOBY will probably collapse honestly. (Also, please come to HOBY Alaska with me next year – or just any other HOBY with me.)

2). Also the fact that we had the same major and were both in UTeach at one point??? Iconic. We're basically the same person. However, I hope you COMPLETE UTeach and go on to be an English teacher! I'm currently looking into alternative ways to receive my certification – so definitely finish it. I don't regret not finishing, but I do wish I had the certification. Plus, you'd be, like, a kickass teacher – just like your mom is.

3). YOU'RE IN KD. Kappa Delta is literally my favorite sorority on UT's campus and I can't believe you're in it! Have so much fun in it. One of my only regrets in regard to university is the fact that I didn't get involved in Greek Life more. So make the most of it and have fun!!!!!

Anyway, I really appreciate you a whole lot. I hope to get to know you even better from here on out! Seriously. Don't be afraid to contact me at the below information. xo.

Sincerely,
Austin James Robinson

[NAME REDACTED],

If you're reading this, it's because you 'liked' or 'reacted' to a Facebook status I made back in April. I know, it's been awhile and I suck! I expect you to expect me to send you the Cheesecake Factory Menu or something – and honestly I will do that at a later time if you wish, – but this is a letter containing things I appreciate about you.

1). The fact that we met because of [REDACTED] when I was running against the [REDACTED] you were helping out with, yet somehow we still became friends. You became one of those people I was excited to see while [REDACTED], and everyone else was probably like, "Wtf – aren't they on different [REDACTED]??" Amazing.

2). How dedicated you are to [REDACTED]. You and, like, several other of my friends are so dedicated and in love with [REDACTED] that it makes me wish I would have attended or at least helped out with it! To have so many people in my life who believe in the mission of [REDACTED] to the point of it almost being a cult definitely has me shook and regretting that I never got involved.

3). Your sense of humor. You are incredibly funny in your day-to-day life – you don't even have to try. And I think that's what I really enjoyed about you (and that was IT – NOTHING ELSE).

Anyway, I really appreciate you a whole lot. I hope to get to know you even better from here on out! Seriously. Don't be afraid to contact me at the below information. xo.

Sincerely,
Austin James Robinson

[NAME REDACTED],

If you're reading this, it's because you 'liked' or 'reacted' to a Facebook status I made back in April. I know, it's been awhile and I suck! I expect you to expect me to send you the Cheesecake Factory Menu or something – and honestly I will do that at a later time if you wish, – but this is a letter containing things I appreciate about you.

1). How you invited me to the Our Three Brothers vigil. It was an intense experience to be mourning the loss (#RestInPower) with you and given the honor holding a sign for everyone to see. It was a powerful, yet difficult moment, and I'm glad I got to be there in solidarity. Thank you for giving me that understanding, and the ability to hear wonderful poetry honoring them and prayers being lifted up in their honor. I will never forget that.

2). How you wholeheartedly supported mine and Daniel's Student Government Executive Alliance campaign. You were one of our most faithful supporters, and I cannot thank you enough for believing in us and what we stood for. Although we didn't win, with people like you it still feels like we made a difference.

Anyway, I really appreciate you a whole lot. I hope to get to know you even better from here on out! Seriously. Don't be afraid to contact me at the below information. xo.

Sincerely,
Austin James Robinson

Nancy Huang,

If you're reading this, it's because you 'liked' or 'reacted' to a Facebook status I made back in April. I know, it's been awhile and I suck! I expect you to expect me to send you the Cheesecake Factory Menu or something – and honestly I will do that at a later time if you wish, – but this is a letter containing things I appreciate about you.

1). Our times during Study Abroad! I know we didn't hang out too much during our time in England, but we still hung out and you were pretty cool! I'm glad we got to connect and add each other on Facebook, and see each other around campus! I remember one time I saw you hanging out in the spot above 7-Eleven, which I appreciated because I feel like that's a pretty secret spot. However, I didn't say hi because you had your earphones in ☹

2). Your poetry. I am so happy you are putting your poetry out there and submitting it and even making a freaking book! It's really good and I'm glad you're a writer who isn't afraid to open up to everyone and show them what kind of skills you have in regard to writing. I know a lot of people who will never show their poetry (I'm still trying to get over that fear), so this is huge. I would love to read your book one day, and I hope you never stop writing poetry.

Anyway, I really appreciate you a whole lot. I hope to get to know you even better from here on out! Seriously. Don't be afraid to contact me at the below information. xo.

Sincerely,
Austin James Robinson

PROJECT LETTERS

Nathaniel Belachew,

If you're reading this, it's because you 'liked' or 'reacted' to a Facebook status I made back in April. I know, it's been awhile and I suck! I expect you to expect me to send you the Cheesecake Factory Menu or something – and honestly I will do that at a later time if you wish, – but this is a letter containing things I appreciate about you.

1). The fact that you're from Canada. I know this is, like, against your control, so it's probably not something I should absolutely appreciate about you, but you know that my family is from Canada, so I guess we gotta APPRECIATE EACH OTHER. Likewise, don't you have, like, triple citizenship?

2). Your personality. I know what you're thinking: "Wow, what a very original point to make!" But you know what I mean. You have a pretty unique personality – I know so many people love you in APO and you make them laugh. And your Facebook game is (or was, I kind of fell off of the face of earth on Facebook [and APO] and now I don't know much) strong af (hundred hundred hundred).

3). Remember when we went to the Dell Children's Medical Center to do BINGO with children? That was really fun. I wish I would have stayed in APO to have more times like that with you, but OH WELL.

Anyway, I really appreciate you a whole lot. I hope to get to know you even better from here on out! Seriously. Don't be afraid to contact me at the below information. xo.

Sincerely,
Austin James Robinson

Nicholas Cobb,

If you're reading this, it's because you 'liked' or 'reacted' to a Facebook status I made back in April. I know, it's been awhile and I suck! I expect you to expect me to send you the Cheesecake Factory Menu or something – and honestly I will do that at a later time if you wish, – but this is a letter containing things I appreciate about you.

1). Your meme game. We know you were the original meme-maker well before any of those fools over at UT Memes and Blah Blah Whatever (dumb-ass page). Without you, there would be no meme game at the University of Texas. I hope Joseph Bae credits you. Anyway, thanks for always posting memes on my things and remaking my shit into memes and whatnot!

2). Your loyalty to my brand. Man, you're always buying my shit when I come out with new stuff. Someday I'm going to sell, like, an airplane and you'll want it. And that's what I've always loved about you. I look forward to working with you when I literally sell every single product there is in the world.

3). How dedicated you are to UDems. When I think of UDems, I basically just think of you, Cheyenne Brown, and a couple of other people, and anti-Student Government. Amazing. Keep doing great work over there.

Anyway, I really appreciate you a whole lot. I hope to get to know you even better from here on out! Seriously. Don't be afraid to contact me at the below information. xo.

Sincerely,
Austin James Robinson

Nick Langston,

If you're reading this, it's because you 'liked' or 'reacted' to a Facebook status I made back in April. I know, it's been awhile and I suck! I expect you to expect me to send you the Cheesecake Factory Menu or something – and honestly I will do that at a later time if you wish, – but this is a letter containing things I appreciate about you.

1). The fact that we met at HOBY in Arkansas and that you're the only person who I still talk to from there. That was such a weird time for me. It was the first HOBY outside of the state of Texas that I was volunteering for (also the first HOBY that was in a hotel), so I was pretty out of place. And I'm glad we became friends. I still wish you would have went to the University of Texas at Austin to do Computer Science, but University of Tulsa seems pretty cool, too! And I'm so happy that I got to go there and visit you! I wanna do that again!

2). How passionate you are about Juggling. That's really freaking cool – you're the only person I know in my entire life who juggles and does competitions and goes to festivals and all that jazz. Iconic. And I've even picked up some Juggling lingo because of you. I swear one day I'm going to go to one of those Juggling festivals that you keep telling me about.

Anyway, I really appreciate you a whole lot. I hope to get to know you even better from here on out! Seriously. Don't be afraid to contact me at the below information. xo.

Sincerely,
Austin James Robinson

Niki Simonsen,

If you're reading this, it's because you 'liked' or 'reacted' to a Facebook status I made back in April. I know, it's been awhile and I suck! I expect you to expect me to send you the Cheesecake Factory Menu or something – and honestly I will do that at a later time if you wish, – but this is a letter containing things I appreciate about you.

1). When we went to Stanford together for that JSA Summer School thing. Honestly, I was never in JSA, so I had no clue what I was getting myself into. But I remember you being pretty cool and exceptionally funny. You're definitely one of the few people I remember from that. However, we haven't really talked AT ALL since then. I'm having a hard time finding things to say to you. So, I'm just going to tell you a story:

2). This one time I walked in on a naked cop while he was masturbating in his own home. Yeah, none of that probably makes sense to you. Me neither. But essentially I was picking up my friend's friend who didn't have a phone capable of calling and had only given me her address. For some reason, there were three houses back-to-back that all had the same exact address. So of course I went to the first one! When she texted me, "Come to the back!" she meant the back house, not the back of the first house. But of course I went straight into that house and walked to the back, and there he was, naked and masturbating. I found out later that he was a cop. Anyway, I hope that was fun for you to read and not disgusting and embarrassing at all!

Anyway, I really appreciate you a whole lot. I hope to get to know you even better from here on out! Seriously. Don't be afraid to contact me at the below information. xo.

Sincerely,
Austin James Robinson

[NAME REDACTED],

If you're reading this, it's because you 'liked' or 'reacted' to a Facebook status I made back in April. I know, it's been awhile and I suck! I expect you to expect me to send you the Cheesecake Factory Menu or something – and honestly I will do that at a later time if you wish, – but this is a letter containing things I appreciate about you.

1). Being in [REDACTED] with you. I know I wasn't in it for that long at all, but I remember you always being one of the nicest people I had met through that [REDACTED]. Your personality is glowing, and I love that. I'm sorry that we didn't get to know each other better, and I'm not about to attempt to reach for a 250-word letter based solely on our limited time together in [REDACTED]. So here's a story instead!

2). There's been two separate times that I've accidentally found myself at a screamo concert. The first time I was just strolling around the local park with a friend when we heard really loud music, people screaming, and the sounds of heads being banged against concrete. Sounds like The Purge, right? Well, that's kind of what a screamo concert is like. I was in middle school, so of course I was wearing Hollister and cargo shorts. We walked up to the concert and decided to stay anyway, even though I looked so out of place. It was fun! The second time was at a local church. I guess Christian Screamo is a thing, and I found myself smack-dab in the middle of that thing. Now, there was a lot of opposition to this in the community – a lot of Christian mothers believe that screamo is the music of the devil. As if the devil came down and legitimately handed us screamo music. Anyway, I think I've learned my lesson because I haven't stumbled upon a screamo concert since.

Anyway, I really appreciate you a whole lot. I hope to get to know you even better from here on out! Seriously. Don't be afraid to contact me at the below information. xo.

Sincerely,
Austin James Robinson

Patrick Campbell,

If you're reading this, it's because you 'liked' or 'reacted' to a Facebook status I made back in April. I know, it's been awhile and I suck! I expect you to expect me to send you the Cheesecake Factory Menu or something – and honestly I will do that at a later time if you wish, – but this is a letter containing things I appreciate about you.

1). Your personality. Everyone loves you in APO. At least when I was in it. I guess, technically, everyone could hate you now, considering I'm no longer in APO and, thus, have no clue what's going on anymore. Anyway, this is off-topic now. I'm SURE they still love you (but sorry if this is false now. Oops).

2). Oh shit, I didn't even address your personality. So, you're SO nice and incredibly outgoing (even though I think you consider yourself pretty introverted – I think it just took a group of 200 friends to make you outgoing, but maybe I'm talking out of my ass now). You're willing to be friends with anyone and everyone, a trait not found in many people at all. Keep loving.

3). Your poetry. Some fucking good shit, dude. HUNDRED. Keep doing it. And maybe publish it someday! Seriously.

Anyway, I really appreciate you a whole lot. I hope to get to know you even better from here on out! Seriously. Don't be afraid to contact me at the below information. xo.

Sincerely,
Austin James Robinson

Patrick Golden,

If you're reading this, it's because you 'liked' or 'reacted' to a Facebook status I made back in April. I know, it's been awhile and I suck! I expect you to expect me to send you the Cheesecake Factory Menu or something – and honestly I will do that at a later time if you wish, – but this is a letter containing things I appreciate about you.

1). How OUT THERE you are. The stories you tell me about what you do baffle me and make me want to force you to write a book immediately. And I thought that I had crazy stories; when I hear your stories, it makes me want to literally start life over and do it right. Never stop creating stories.

2). The fact that we've done so many different cool-ass things that I cannot sit here and fully comprehend or think of a list to make. We've cooked at a Buddhist Temple, we've gone to Orgasmic Therapy, we've almost done Air Sex together, we've illegally floated the Guadalupe river together at 3am and almost died when we had 8ams the next day (I didn't end up attending class), we've walked the dead streets of Fredericksburg until a cop told us to leave, etc. And that's just, like, a small portion of what we've done. Wait, I just remembered when we stayed at a hostel literally right next to my apartment complex – so we just had to walk to it and walk back in the morning. That was fucking fun. Why haven't we done a road trip together? Soon.

Anyway, I really appreciate you a whole lot. I hope to get to know you even better from here on out! Seriously. Don't be afraid to contact me at the below information. xo.

Sincerely,
Austin James Robinson

Pedro Corzo,

If you're reading this, it's because you 'liked' or 'reacted' to a Facebook status I made back in April. I know, it's been awhile and I suck! I expect you to expect me to send you the Cheesecake Factory Menu or something – and honestly I will do that at a later time if you wish, – but this is a letter containing things I appreciate about you.

1). Your fame in the gay community. I have no clue how, but every time I make a gay friend in Austin, you're automatically a mutual friend between us. Iconic. You could lead us as a pack. Be our king. Literally create an event and every gay would go. I look forward to attending. xo

2). The fact that you went to Coats On A Boat with [REDACTED]. I'm so sorry to bring him up because I know y'all are done, but I do so just to say that I have never seen a gay couple at a Texas Blazers event. Even the gays currently in Texas Blazers just take girls – it's kind of dumb. I was really happy to see gay representation in an org that is highly heteronormative.

3). A third thing! Idk, we never talked much – and barely ever in person. But we should talk more! I can't even remember your major or anything! But I can't wait to see what you do in life.

Anyway, I really appreciate you a whole lot. I hope to get to know you even better from here on out! Seriously. Don't be afraid to contact me at the below information. xo.

Sincerely,
Austin James Robinson

Priya Suri,

If you're reading this, it's because you 'liked' or 'reacted' to a Facebook status I made back in April. I know, it's been awhile and I suck! I expect you to expect me to send you the Cheesecake Factory Menu or something – and honestly I will do that at a later time if you wish, – but this is a letter containing things I appreciate about you.

1). The fact that you're in Texas Spirits! CONGRATULATIONS ON BECOMING ACTIVE AND GETTING YOUR SCARF!!! Now we're basically organizational siblings! I mean, I sort of think of Texas Blazers and Texas Spirits as the same organization already. So, really, where is the line? I say it's pretty blurry. Maybe we're the same person? This is a conspiracy theory at this point. I digress. You're gonna change the world someday. Keep serving people AND looks!

2). How dedicated you are to Student Government. Or at least, were. I know you were Liberal Arts Representative, but I actually graduated in December of 2016, so I have no clue if you're still involved or not. Regardless, you kick ass when it comes to being involved at UT! You are definitely one of the star students, and I cannot wait to see what you do for the university and the world!

Anyway, I really appreciate you a whole lot. I hope to get to know you even better from here on out! Seriously. Don't be afraid to contact me at the below information. xo.

Sincerely,
Austin James Robinson

Racheile Ricklefs,

If you're reading this, it's because you 'liked' or 'reacted' to a Facebook status I made back in April. I know, it's been awhile and I suck! I expect you to expect me to send you the Cheesecake Factory Menu or something – and honestly I will do that at a later time if you wish, – but this is a letter containing things I appreciate about you.

1). That time we met at the Circle K International Convention in, I think, Indianapolis. I say *I think* because I literally cannot remember anything. But I remember you winning International President, and I thought that was pretty cool because you're a really nice and awesome person and I wouldn't have wanted anyone else to win. Anyway, I'm so glad I met you while I was in CKI!

2). Anyway, we don't really have much else in common / we don't really know each other, so do you want to hear about my history with hamsters? Okay, so my first hamster was when I was in elementary school. It took the wood chips and trapped itself inside of the tube structure and then suffocated. Then there was the time I owned two hamsters in middle school. One of them ate the other one and murdered it. So I just got rid of them. Then I bought a hamster that had developmental disabilities. Actually, the guy sort of just gave it to me for free because it was going to "die anyway." And it did. That night. The final time I was around hamsters was when my roommate in university threw her hamsters off of the third-story balcony because she didn't know how else to rid herself of the responsibility. The end.

Anyway, I really appreciate you a whole lot. I hope to get to know you even better from here on out! Seriously. Don't be afraid to contact me at the below information. xo.

Sincerely,
Austin James Robinson

PROJECT LETTERS

Reid Luedecke,

If you're reading this, it's because you 'liked' or 'reacted' to a Facebook status I made back in April. I know, it's been awhile and I suck! I expect you to expect me to send you the Cheesecake Factory Menu or something – and honestly I will do that at a later time if you wish, – but this is a letter containing things I appreciate about you.

1). Actually, you know what? I'm just going to tell you a story. Okay, so you know how I met you at the on-campus Queens of Texas drag show back in, like, forever ago? Okay, so the four friends I was with were all dating each other. (Not, like, some big polyamorous thing, but they were two sets of relationships.) And I just talk to everyone, so naturally you and me were chatting. Well, suddenly in the middle of the show, they all leave and text me to say, "We left so you could have some alone time with Reid." Which is already weird and awkward because I don't even know how to tie my shoes let alone talk to a guy! (Okay, I do know how to tie my shoes, but just imagine for the purpose of this hyperbolized retelling of the event.) Anyway, they wanted me to be with you or something, but the most exciting thing that happened that night was the fact that I lost my wallet at the drag show and had to go all the way back to the SAC ballroom in order to retrieve it.

2). Okay, I guess I'll include something I actually like about you: I love how service-oriented you are. From volunteering with Rotaract to taking courses in health-related fields, you seem like you definitely want to help make the world a better place, and that's hot. Don't stop that.

Anyway, I really appreciate you a whole lot. I hope to get to know you even better from here on out! Seriously. Don't be afraid to contact me at the below information. xo.

Sincerely,
Austin James Robinson

Rene Gonzalez,

If you're reading this, it's because you 'liked' or 'reacted' to a Facebook status I made back in April. I know, it's been awhile and I suck! I expect you to expect me to send you the Cheesecake Factory Menu or something – and honestly I will do that at a later time if you wish, – but this is a letter containing things I appreciate about you.

1). How quick you were to become my friend in Circle K International. You, Fabian, and Courtney were basically my only friends in CKI my entire time in there, so when y'all left I was pretty sad and basically quit hahaha. But during that time, you were so cool. You were the first person I was really able to discuss underground music with. I come from a place where everyone basically just listens to the radio, so it was so surreal for me to meet someone who was into music as much (if not more) as I was.

2). Your sense of style. Your outfits are always perfect. Ever since I can remember. I don't have much to say about this – just keep doing it. Also, remember when we volunteered at that Women's Shelter Garage Sale together? Prime fashion.

3). YOU'RE A NURSE. Loves it. Maybe you'll be my nurse someday. Wait, that would mean I would be sick. Maybe I'll hire you as a nurse to do nothing?? Idk, we'll talk about it. Just let me know what you think about this idea.

Anyway, I really appreciate you a whole lot. I hope to get to know you even better from here on out! Seriously. Don't be afraid to contact me at the below information. xo.

Sincerely,
Austin James Robinson

[NAME REDACTED],

If you're reading this, it's because you 'liked' or 'reacted' to a Facebook status I made back in April. I know, it's been awhile and I suck! I expect you to expect me to send you the Cheesecake Factory Menu or something – and honestly I will do that at a later time if you wish, – but this is a letter containing things I appreciate about you.

1). THE FACT THAT YOU'RE IN [REDACTED]. I can't remember whether or not you were in [REDACTED], but I bet you were considering most [REDACTED] members only know about it because of being in [REDACTED]. But I'm so happy we were both apart of [REDACTED] because it's such a grand organization that is definitely underappreciated. I graduated from it and now I'm in [REDACTED] (which I hope you'll be in), but I hope you make the most out of it while you're still in it!

2). How supportive you are of my brand. I remember when you bought a t-shirt from me and took a picture with it on and then it ended up on a pretty popular Tumblr page! It was so surreal to receive a text message from one of my good friends saying that they had just saw someone wearing my t-shirt on Tumblr! Amazing. Thank you so much.

Anyway, I really appreciate you a whole lot. I hope to get to know you even better from here on out! Seriously. Don't be afraid to contact me at the below information. xo.

Sincerely,
Austin James Robinson

Robert Orr,

If you're reading this, it's because you 'liked' or 'reacted' to a Facebook status I made back in April. I know, it's been awhile and I suck! I expect you to expect me to send you the Cheesecake Factory Menu or something – and honestly I will do that at a later time if you wish, – but this is a letter containing things I appreciate about you.

1). How we used to play Pokémon together back when I was, like, 5-years-old. And now we're still 5-years-old and we still play Pokémon (oh just me?). But seriously, can you imagine the journey we've gone on? I mean, you were there, but also can you imagine it? I can't believe we became good friends at the tale end of high school (for me). And then we sort of chatted throughout university because of Circle K International. And now we just got done chaperoning a convention together and drinking alcohol in that park in the middle of Dallas. I can't wait to see where I hang out with you unexpectedly next.

2). Your glow-up. I've always thought you were cute. I think I've had a crush on you since before I can remember. But shit – you were such a fucking nerd-looking kid for the longest time. Now you suddenly look like the hottest CEO of a huge Fortune 500 company or some shit? Nice.

Anyway, I really appreciate you a whole lot. I hope to get to know you even better from here on out! Seriously. Don't be afraid to contact me at the below information. xo.

Sincerely,
Austin James Robinson

PROJECT LETTERS

Ron Matan,

If you're reading this, it's because you 'liked' or 'reacted' to a Facebook status I made back in April. I know, it's been awhile and I suck! I expect you to expect me to send you the Cheesecake Factory Menu or something – and honestly I will do that at a later time if you wish, – but this is a letter containing things I appreciate about you.

1). How we met on a dating app and immediately added each other on Facebook. Then you sent me, "Who are you?" and my reply to you was literally, "Grindr guy!" And I like knowing that I'm "Grindr Guy" in your life. That is literally my identifier. Well, until you found out about my brand and then started asking me tons of questions about that, which leads me to my next point:

2). Your support of my brand and the weird shit that I do. I remember after I told you about the brand beginning and all of the products that I sell and do, you were kind of wow'd by it. And you were very nice in your responses. Let's collaborate someday! I love doing projects with other people. Tell me what you're good at, and we'll do something.

Anyway, I really appreciate you a whole lot. I hope to get to know you even better from here on out! Seriously. Don't be afraid to contact me at the below information. xo.

Sincerely,
Austin James Robinson

Ryan Floyd,

If you're reading this, it's because you 'liked' or 'reacted' to a Facebook status I made back in April. I know, it's been awhile and I suck! I expect you to expect me to send you the Cheesecake Factory Menu or something – and honestly I will do that at a later time if you wish, – but this is a letter containing things I appreciate about you.

1). The fact that we met in Saint John, New Brunswick during Pride Week (I think it was around that time, or at least a little after). I'm glad we got to hang out at Queen's Park (or King's – one of those) and then go to the Fringe Film Festival together to see the Canadian improv version of HAMILTON. And then of course I got to see your musical! Which brings me to my next point...

2). How you've totally written and starred in many of YOUR OWN plays / musicals! That's so amazing. I'm not sure if they're all on the web, but I would love to be able to see them all one day from the comfort of my own home! Keep on creating. I will always watch.

3). That time we made out basically on top of a urinal. That was really fun and honestly an underrated place to make out. More people should make out on top of urinals. It's an experience if nothing else.

Anyway, I really appreciate you a whole lot. I hope to get to know you even better from here on out! Seriously. Don't be afraid to contact me at the below information. xo.

Sincerely,
Austin James Robinson

Ryan Mullowney,

If you're reading this, it's because you 'liked' or 'reacted' to a Facebook status I made back in April. I know, it's been awhile and I suck! I expect you to expect me to send you the Cheesecake Factory Menu or something – and honestly I will do that at a later time if you wish, – but this is a letter containing things I appreciate about you.

1). The fact that you have more life experience than, like, me and all of our mutual friends. You were probably the most mature person in all of APO, so I apologize on behalf of everyone in it for being dumb and dramatic, lmaooooo. But it was so great to have YOU as my little even though you're bigger than me, and to be one of your good friends in the organization, and beyond it. I wanna keep that up.

2). How similar we are in our thought process and opinions. We've had MANY conversations about society and politics, and every time, we typically agree with each other. Our personalities are wildly different, but we are such similar people – it's amazing. I love that.

3). Our book. Or lack there-of, so far. We have had a book idea circulating between us for, what, two years now? At least we have the outline complete. I feel like once we just start, it'll be no time before we complete it. Let's do it. I want to publish it before the year's end.

Anyway, I really appreciate you a whole lot. I hope to get to know you even better from here on out! Seriously. Don't be afraid to contact me at the below information. xo.

Sincerely,
Austin James Robinson

Sammy Lutes,

If you're reading this, it's because you 'liked' or 'reacted' to a Facebook status I made back in April. I know, it's been awhile and I suck! I expect you to expect me to send you the Cheesecake Factory Menu or something – and honestly I will do that at a later time if you wish, – but this is a letter containing things I appreciate about you.

1). How absolutely positive you are no matter how your day is going. Literally, I feel like everything bad in the world could be happening to you, but you would still have a smile on your face for every person you came into contact with. You are just the most happy and positive person I know. Thank you for that. I don't even know how it's possible to be more positive than me, but I'm glad someone's doing it.

2). The time at UT we spent together (mainly in Alpha Phi Omega). I really miss seeing you. You were hilarious and weren't afraid to be yourself. Why'd you have to leave ☹☹☹

3). How every gay guy seems to love you. Literally, I have had multiple gay guys tell me that they just wish you were gay. And I've even felt that way before. What is it about you that makes all of the gays love you? Amazing.

Anyway, I really appreciate you a whole lot. I hope to get to know you even better from here on out! Seriously. Don't be afraid to contact me at the below information. xo.

Sincerely,
Austin James Robinson

Samuel Garcia,

If you're reading this, it's because you 'liked' or 'reacted' to a Facebook status I made back in April. I know, it's been awhile and I suck! I expect you to expect me to send you the Cheesecake Factory Menu or something – and honestly I will do that at a later time if you wish, – but this is a letter containing things I appreciate about you.

1). Okay, I actually kind of want to tell you a story instead: remember when we first met? It was in Christina Boatman's FIG class thing and I said hi to you and you basically ignored me. And then a couple weeks later, you were headed to the Alpha Phi Omega office, and I said hi to you AND YOU IGNORED ME. Then I guess you got wind that I was the individual who has the most service houses in APO in the entire nation, and suddenly YOU LOVED ME. Wow. Is that all it TOOK? So the third time I saw you, I was walking past the APO table on Greg Plaza (I think y'all were giving out candy for finals or something), and you literally bombarded me about how I'm a LEGEND. Wow, we've come a long way. I'm glad you've finally decided to start talking to me!

2). In that same note, I'm actually very glad that now you are the individual who is quickly becoming the person to have the most service hours ever. I seriously dare you to garner more service hours than me in your APO lifetime. It shouldn't be too hard considering I left APO after 3 semesters. So come back to me when you've done that.

Anyway, I really appreciate you a whole lot. I hope to get to know you even better from here on out! Seriously. Don't be afraid to contact me at the below information. xo.

Sincerely,
Austin James Robinson

Sara Harpole,

If you're reading this, it's because you 'liked' or 'reacted' to a Facebook status I made back in April. I know, it's been awhile and I suck! I expect you to expect me to send you the Cheesecake Factory Menu or something – and honestly I will do that at a later time if you wish, – but this is a letter containing things I appreciate about you.

1). The fact that we went to Texas Business Summer whatever together. I mean, we only really talked to each other once when our two teams met in the same classroom. Also, I ultimately ended up dropping out of that program and living in Los Angeles for the remainder of the time, anyway. Also, other than that, we really don't know each other that well :/ Besides sort of being in YAL together (which you were a major member of and I just kind of joined because I was actually technically in every single political organization on campus). So I guess I can't really say much about why I appreciate you ☹ Do you want to hear about the times I was in ISS in public school? Is this enough of a distraction? Okay!

2). The first time was in 7th grade and my tennis coach was saying that I sounded like Michael Jackson. He meant this as some weird form of an insult. So I said, "Fuck you!" And then I got ISS. The next and only other time was in 8th grade when we were supposed to write a poem about society for English class. I wrote about how men are always obsessed with their dicks and women are obsessed with their boobs. And my teacher didn't really like that, so I went to ISS. Thanks for listening!

Anyway, I really appreciate you a whole lot. I hope to get to know you even better from here on out! Seriously. Don't be afraid to contact me at the below information. xo.

Sincerely,
Austin James Robinson

Sara Leonard,

If you're reading this, it's because you 'liked' or 'reacted' to a Facebook status I made back in April. I know, it's been awhile and I suck! I expect you to expect me to send you the Cheesecake Factory Menu or something – and honestly I will do that at a later time if you wish, – but this is a letter containing things I appreciate about you.

1). The fact that we met during Study Abroad in England and somehow would have definitely met regardless of that. Remember how we mainly talked about Big Brother US during Study Abroad (but never really watched it together for some reason). And then I matched with that Big Brother UK winner on Tinder. And then a couple of other people from Study Abroad also loved Big Brother so we would make fake Big Brother games on the web together. Wtf, who were we?

2). How dedicated you are to Senate of College Councils and Orange Jackets. We became even more connected when me and your boyfriend met in Texas Blazers (that was actually a very glorious moment). And then when I sort of scammed my way onto the President Student Advisory Council representing Senate and spent so much time in the office that you were probably hella annoyed. Then you became an Orange Jacket and you got to see me even more! Wow, aren't you glad all of this happened?

Anyway, I really appreciate you a whole lot. I hope to get to know you even better from here on out! Seriously. Don't be afraid to contact me at the below information. xo.

Sincerely,
Austin James Robinson

Sarah Brashear,

If you're reading this, it's because you 'liked' or 'reacted' to a Facebook status I made back in April. I know, it's been awhile and I suck! I expect you to expect me to send you the Cheesecake Factory Menu or something – and honestly I will do that at a later time if you wish, – but this is a letter containing things I appreciate about you.

1). The fact that you're dating DJ Roberts. Remember how I've called him "Robert" literally three different times that I've run into you? Honestly, none of those times were on purpose. I swear I really love him and that I consider him a friend, so I have no clue why running into you makes me momentarily forget his name. Oh well!

2). How you're in Texas Spirits AND Orange Jackets? How do you do that?? I got denied to BOTH. But seriously, you give so much of yourself to others, and it's really beautiful. Keep changing the freaking world.

3). Do you want to hear a story about how the Drive-Thru cashier at a popular fast food chain thought I was a woman based on my voice? He kept calling me "ma'am" (which I honestly don't care about), but then when he saw me at the payment window, he began to say "man" as if he could totally get away with it! Whatatwist!

Anyway, I really appreciate you a whole lot. I hope to get to know you even better from here on out! Seriously. Don't be afraid to contact me at the below information. xo.

Sincerely,
Austin James Robinson

PROJECT LETTERS

Sean Burris,

If you're reading this, it's because you 'liked' or 'reacted' to a Facebook status I made back in April. I know, it's been awhile and I suck! I expect you to expect me to send you the Cheesecake Factory Menu or something – and honestly I will do that at a later time if you wish, – but this is a letter containing things I appreciate about you.

1). How we met, like, three years ago at the Circle K International Convention (I think because we were in the same volunteering group) and still sort of talk to this day – well, at least we're still friends on Facebook. I'm sure we're both graduated now, but I've totally joined Kiwanis now that I'm an OLD MAN.

2). How you aren't afraid to comment on my posts and ask for free stuff, lmao. I just recently sent you my ghostwritten book. I know we discussed combining this letter with that book, so I'm really sorry I wrote this so late. But it's pretty cool that you're interested in my posts and my content. Literally ask for whatever and I'll probably do it, honestly.

3). How into flying you are. I, like, want to get my pilot's license, but I have NO clue what I'd do with it afterwards. I can't do anything in the Air Force because I don't have 20/20 vision or whatever is required. And I'm not sure I'd absolutely love being a pilot for, like, Delta or whatever. But I'm glad I get to live vicariously through you!

Anyway, I really appreciate you a whole lot. I hope to get to know you even better from here on out! Seriously. Don't be afraid to contact me at the below information. xo.

Sincerely,
Austin James Robinson

[NAME REDACTED],

If you're reading this, it's because you 'liked' or 'reacted' to a Facebook status I made back in April. I know, it's been awhile and I suck! I expect you to expect me to send you the Cheesecake Factory Menu or something – and honestly I will do that at a later time if you wish, – but this is a letter containing things I appreciate about you.

1). The fact that you go to [REDACTED], and that's one of my favorite places. I know I go to the [REDACTED] so I'm, like, supposed to hate you or something? Idk – the rules are a little weird in that regard. But, yeah, I have so many friends at [REDACTED] and I've been there so many times. I want to get a [REDACTED] there or something. I don't even know – I just want to go there. Hahaha. SO THANKS FOR MAKING ME FEEL CLOSER TO THE [REDACTED].

2). How we met at [REDACTED]. Not to bring [REDACTED] back up, but [REDACTED] is probably the best [REDACTED] I've ever met and witnessed. I'm so glad I was in [REDACTED] long enough to meet y'all and serve with you. I hope you continue to make a difference in the world!

Anyway, I really appreciate you a whole lot. I hope to get to know you even better from here on out! Seriously. Don't be afraid to contact me at the below information. xo.

Sincerely,
Austin James Robinson

[NAME REDACTED],

If you're reading this, it's because you 'liked' or 'reacted' to a Facebook status I made back in April. I know, it's been awhile and I suck! I expect you to expect me to send you the Cheesecake Factory Menu or something – and honestly I will do that at a later time if you wish, – but this is a letter containing things I appreciate about you.

1). How we met in the [REDACTED] office and now we're here. Do you remember when we met? I thought you were really cute, so I kept asking you questions and then we talked about how cool [REDACTED] is and your [REDACTED]. Anyway, it's pretty cool to look back on the journey that is our friendship. I hope it goes on forever.

2). The fact that you're my [REDACTED] in [REDACTED]. I'm so happy that you joined [REDACTED]. I was literally going to force them to accept you regardless, so you would have gotten in no matter what. But what's even crazier is that you became my [REDACTED]. And then we immediately began taking pictures with [REDACTED] – so if that doesn't tell you how perfect of a match we are, I don't know what will. I guess now that I'm graduated, you're technically [REDACTED]. Sorry!

3). How I feel about you. But you already know.

Anyway, I really appreciate you a whole lot. I hope to get to know you even better from here on out! Seriously. Don't be afraid to contact me at the below information. xo.

Sincerely,
Austin James Robinson

Shane Colwell,

If you're reading this, it's because you 'liked' or 'reacted' to a Facebook status I made back in April. I know, it's been awhile and I suck! I expect you to expect me to send you the Cheesecake Factory Menu or something – and honestly I will do that at a later time if you wish, – but this is a letter containing things I appreciate about you.

1). How we matched on Tinder and made plans to watch shows together, but never did. I know this sounds like an odd thing to appreciate about another person – I mean, aren't we, as human beings and social creatures, supposed to go through with plans and actually execute them to ensure trusting relationships build and develop? Well, that's where I say WRONG. Because who's to say we didn't DEVELOP and TRUST our relationship because we ignored the potentiality (word?) of becoming closer? Checkmate.

2). How you're friends with [REDACTED]. I know this seems like another weird thing I would appreciate about you, but he's a really good guy, and I'm glad to know that one of our mutual friends (sort of – he kind of hates me) is someone like [REDACTED]. Wow, was this point even about you? Am I total dick who is dodging all of these points that are supposed to be good things about YOU? Who can never be sure.

Anyway, I really appreciate you a whole lot. I hope to get to know you even better from here on out! Seriously. Don't be afraid to contact me at the below information. xo.

Sincerely,
Austin James Robinson

[NAME REDACTED],

If you're reading this, it's because you 'liked' or 'reacted' to a Facebook status I made back in April. I know, it's been awhile and I suck! I expect you to expect me to send you the Cheesecake Factory Menu or something – and honestly I will do that at a later time if you wish, – but this is a letter containing things I appreciate about you.

1). Your sense of humor. You are so fucking funny and original. I remember when you had that YouTube channel called, like, [REDACTED] or something like that. First of all: iconic name. Second of all: I showed your videos to literally dozens of my friends and they absolutely loved them. I was devastated when you deleted the channel.

2). I say this one with extreme caution: The fact that I think MAYBE possibly you're being ironic about being [REDACTED]. Like, either way: cool. But me and several people have had the conversation that we can never tell if you're being sincere or ironic when you talk about [REDACTED] on social media. If you're being sincere, awesome. If you're being ironic, it is one of the best ironic endeavors I have ever experienced.

3). How much you stayed true to yourself throughout high school (and now). I know this sounds like a dumb point, but I just remember you being yourself and not caring what other people thought (and I believe you still do this). I admired that because there definitely wasn't a lot of people like that in our high school.

Anyway, I really appreciate you a whole lot. I hope to get to know you even better from here on out! Seriously. Don't be afraid to contact me at the below information. xo.

Sincerely,
Austin James Robinson

[NAME REDACTED],

If you're reading this, it's because you 'liked' or 'reacted' to a Facebook status I made back in April. I know, it's been awhile and I suck! I expect you to expect me to send you the Cheesecake Factory Menu or something – and honestly I will do that at a later time if you wish, – but this is a letter containing things I appreciate about you.

1). The fact that we met in [REDACTED] and you were a pretty cool and popular member. I wasn't in that organization for that long, but you're definitely one of the faces I remember the most. Thanks for serving next to me!!!

2). How you told me about Lynda, that online education service. Honestly, I still haven't utilized it, but I always hear about it and it reminds me how I definitely need to learn some lessons on there (like, Adobe Creative Cloud and stuff). So thanks for initially telling me about it even though I suck at following through with it.

3). The fact that you were one of the first ever people to listen to an AJR song and then immediately message me about how I'm famous and on the radio. You know what's even funnier? That band is composed of three brothers with the first initials of each brother making up the acronym. And my name is Austin, and my brothers' names are Justin and Robbie. I'm not even kidding. We are literally that band.

Anyway, I really appreciate you a whole lot. I hope to get to know you even better from here on out! Seriously. Don't be afraid to contact me at the below information. xo.

Sincerely,
Austin James Robinson

[NAME REDACTED],

If you're reading this, it's because you 'liked' or 'reacted' to a Facebook status I made back in April. I know, it's been awhile and I suck! I expect you to expect me to send you the Cheesecake Factory Menu or something – and honestly I will do that at a later time if you wish, – but this is a letter containing things I appreciate about you.

1). When we had those two [REDACTED] courses together with [REDACTED]. Okay, I totally don't remember the names of those courses at all, and I also remember very little about them. All I know is that you were really funny, I somehow became friends with [REDACTED] afterwards (as he became my [REDACTED] guide), and we all struggled to talk in the courses. Regardless, they were such intimate courses due to the fact that only, about, like, 15 people were in them. Also, now that I'm looking through our Facebook messages, apparently you were my point of contact for anything related to the courses; hahaha. Sorry about that. But also thanks.

2). The fact that you know [REDACTED]. Again, another thing I'm sorry for, but also thankful for. I remember when we found out that we both knew him and it was just the funniest thing ever because he is honestly the most ridiculous person I've ever met.

Anyway, I really appreciate you a whole lot. I hope to get to know you even better from here on out! Seriously. Don't be afraid to contact me at the below information. xo.

Sincerely,
Austin James Robinson

Srikar Nalluri,

If you're reading this, it's because you 'liked' or 'reacted' to a Facebook status I made back in April. I know, it's been awhile and I suck! I expect you to expect me to send you the Cheesecake Factory Menu or something – and honestly I will do that at a later time if you wish, – but this is a letter containing things I appreciate about you.

1). How we met at Stanford University for that JSA Summer School program. And then we both ended up at the University of Texas! Although, I have no clue how I was able to go to that summer program – I had literally never heard of JSA before signing up. Literally, I didn't know what it was about until I was on the Stanford campus and some other student was telling me what we were going to do that summer. Regardless, I'm glad we ended up at the same university! I'm sorry that we never hung out while we were there – I know we both kind of tried to hang out at least once, but it just didn't work out. And now I'm graduated. But let's definitely make up for that and hang out one day! Just let me know when!

2). The fact that you post fire memes in that UT meme page. I hate that group, but you post some pretty good stuff in there. ONE HUNDRED.

Anyway, I really appreciate you a whole lot. I hope to get to know you even better from here on out! Seriously. Don't be afraid to contact me at the below information. xo.

Sincerely,
Austin James Robinson

Stephen Wheadon,

If you're reading this, it's because you 'liked' or 'reacted' to a Facebook status I made back in April. I know, it's been awhile and I suck! I expect you to expect me to send you the Cheesecake Factory Menu or something – and honestly I will do that at a later time if you wish, – but this is a letter containing things I appreciate about you.

1). The fact that we met in Key Club International and have stayed friends since then, even though I hadn't met you for, like, the first four years we knew each other. Thank God for International Convention! That was actually a very fun time, even though I was there for Circle K and you were there for Key Club (okay that makes it sound like I hung out with high school students while in college – I hope you remember that you were working for Key Club and not actually in Key Club at the time).

2). How incredibly thoughtful and nice you are. I don't know many people that will up-and-let me stay with them for an extended period of time, and be sincere about wanting me there. You are willing to let anyone into your home and allow them to stay for as long as they need. Never stop being like that – people really do appreciate it. Also, I'm typing this as I look at the "YOU ROCK!" sticky note that I have on my laptop. It's so dirty and gross now, but if it's gonna come off, it's gonna have to do it on its own.

3). The fact that you work at the Library of Congress. Remember when you snuck me into the underground tunnels and took me to your office? That sounds a lot more secretive and scandalous than I meant it, but I'm keeping it.

Anyway, I really appreciate you a whole lot. I hope to get to know you even better from here on out! Seriously. Don't be afraid to contact me at the below information.

xo.

Sincerely,
Austin James Robinson

UPDATE: The "YOU ROCK!" sticky note literally came off while I was in the process of writing this book, but I taped it back to my computer.

Stewart Schweinfurth,

If you're reading this, it's because you 'liked' or 'reacted' to a Facebook status I made back in April. I know, it's been awhile and I suck! I expect you to expect me to send you the Cheesecake Factory Menu or something – and honestly I will do that at a later time if you wish, – but this is a letter containing things I appreciate about you.

1). The fact that you're fashion conscious. Like, literally, you're so woke when it comes to how to look good. I want every pair of shoes you own. I'm pretty sure that this is the only form of woke that matters.

2). Your sense of humor. You are so peculiar to me – from your general sense of humor to your meme game. I am so perplexed and awed by how much you make different kinds of people laugh. You should be a comedian. Or at least some kind of personality. Just be famous, please.

3). Your ability to think in depth about your life and where you're going. "Dallas is a finish line." You always say this and, combined with everything else we've discussed, it shows that you are willing and wanting to improve yourself and every area of your life constantly.

4). The time we had with Seth in El Paso. Man, that was wild af. Lmao.

Anyway, I really appreciate you a whole lot. I hope to get to know you even better from here on out! Seriously. Don't be afraid to contact me at the below information. xo.

Sincerely,
Austin James Robinson

Stormy Mauldin,

If you're reading this, it's because you 'liked' or 'reacted' to a Facebook status I made back in April. I know, it's been awhile and I suck! I expect you to expect me to send you the Cheesecake Factory Menu or something – and honestly I will do that at a later time if you wish, – but this is a letter containing things I appreciate about you.

1). STORMY. SWAMP G. Man, we have had a rollercoaster of a friendship. You know what I'm talking about. I can't believe we've gone from insults to supporting each other's art. Life is one hell of a ride. But I'm glad we're actually friends now and that we're both doing things that we love, and that we can be ourselves.

2). Your music. You have got to be one of my favorite SoundCloud accounts to follow because your raps are seriously so good and your personality is totally put into your art. I love that. I love your positive raps so much. Keep doing that.

3). How you were valedictorian of your high school and how, for some reason, I was really obsessed with that. You were just so DIFFERENT for being at Early High School. At the time you were a libertarian atheist, and I just thought that was the coolest thing because nobody else held either of those views at all. And you were the smartest student in the school! Always the best at whatever you do.

Anyway, I really appreciate you a whole lot. I hope to get to know you even better from here on out! Seriously. Don't be afraid to contact me at the below information. xo.

Sincerely,
Austin James Robinson

Suhas Tatapudi,

If you're reading this, it's because you 'liked' or 'reacted' to a Facebook status I made back in April. I know, it's been awhile and I suck! I expect you to expect me to send you the Cheesecake Factory Menu or something – and honestly I will do that at a later time if you wish, – but this is a letter containing things I appreciate about you.

1). Your kindness. Dude, you have got to be one of the kindest individuals I have ever met. You are so willing to meet everyone and immediately greet them with open arms – a trait I have not seen in a lot of people. Keep it up.

2). Your dancing abilities. I freaking love Punjabbawockeez, and that video of you doing that one rap dance – something like Juju On The Beat? Idk, but you're fucking hilarious and your dancing is hella great. Not sure if you wanna do it professionally or anything, but I'm glad you're doing it in college!

3). Your love and acceptance of anyone and everyone. I know you go to UT and you're in Texas Blazers and yadda yadda, so it's not a surprise that you're pretty progressive and accepting in your thinking. However, where I come from, this is not the case. So, I am just incredibly grateful to have someone like you in my life who is accepting of me for who I am, and of everyone in your life for who they are. I know we all appreciate this about you.

Anyway, I really appreciate you a whole lot. I hope to get to know you even better from here on out! Seriously. Don't be afraid to contact me at the below information. xo.

Sincerely,
Austin James Robinson

[NAME REDACTED],

If you're reading this, it's because you 'liked' or 'reacted' to a Facebook status I made back in April. I know, it's been awhile and I suck! I expect you to expect me to send you the Cheesecake Factory Menu or something – and honestly I will do that at a later time if you wish, – but this is a letter containing things I appreciate about you.

1). How entirely dedicated you are to each and every organization and cause you are apart of, and the university as a whole. Damn, you do SO MUCH. From [REDACTED] to [REDACTED], you are just everywhere on campus! I cannot even imagine being as active as you, and I feel I'm doing the most! It's quite inspiring and makes me wish I could do university all over again! And then recently how you did [REDACTED] – incredible. Keep doing great things on the campus.

2). Your bubbly and amazing personality. You immediately make everyone feel like your friend, and I absolutely love that. I know we haven't hung out or seen each other around campus much, but I feel like you make it easy to be your friend and know you as a person.

3). Your profile picture game. I don't even need to explain myself here – we all know it.

Anyway, I really appreciate you a whole lot. I hope to get to know you even better from here on out! Seriously. Don't be afraid to contact me at the below information. xo.

Sincerely,
Austin James Robinson

PROJECT LETTERS

Taylor Guerrero,

If you're reading this, it's because you 'liked' or 'reacted' to a Facebook status I made back in April. I know, it's been awhile and I suck! I expect you to expect me to send you the Cheesecake Factory Menu or something – and honestly I will do that at a later time if you wish, – but this is a letter containing things I appreciate about you.

1). Your dedication to Liberal Arts Council. Okay, so I know I was really only in LAC for about a year before you graduated and left (and I was really only in it for a year regardless), but I remember you being one of the most active and outspoken members. I love when people find their place and make the most out of it. But who knows – maybe LAC was just a side thing for you and you happen to just be super passionate about anything you put yourself in (God knows I was not too passionate about LAC, but I was still in it).

2). Your level-headed opinions and thoughts on politics and, really, everything. I remember this one instance when we were eating at a Big Brother Big Sisters (I think – I always get that confused with Boys & Girls Club) track meet, and you were discussing politics with someone. You talked about how people would be quick to jump on a president of the opposed political affiliation as them if they did something they deemed bad, but how they would turn a blind eye to a president of their affiliation for doing the same thing. Does that make sense? I'm sure I'm not bringing it justice, but I loved how you talked about it and seemed completely rational.

3). The fact that you're in law school. Ahhhhh, I could honestly never do it! You're probably literally going to be the best lawyer ever.

Anyway, I really appreciate you a whole lot. I hope to get to know you even better from here on out! Seriously. Don't be afraid to contact me at the below information. xo.

Sincerely,
Austin James Robinson

Teddy Garber,

If you're reading this, it's because you 'liked' or 'reacted' to a Facebook status I made back in April. I know, it's been awhile and I suck! I expect you to expect me to send you the Cheesecake Factory Menu or something – and honestly I will do that at a later time if you wish, – but this is a letter containing things I appreciate about you.

1). How dedicated you were to the Food Recovery Network Dropoff. It was incredibly fun to be able to do that with you and volunteer for it for about a year. I'm not sure what happened to it once you graduated, as I know you were one of the most dedicated members. I'm sorry I couldn't keep doing it once you left! And now I am graduated and gone from Austin. But I always admired how much you were into helping others become food secure. I hope you still serve like you did back then.

2). The fact that you're [REDACTED]'s brother. I love [REDACTED] so much. I remember when I realized he was your brother and me and him were both in [REDACTED] together – amazing. I wish I could have hung out with both of you together! Who knows – technically y'all could be the same person and just be fooling me, considering I've never seen y'all together.

3). Your current educational goals. You're in freaking law school – what the heck. I don't even know what a law is! That's just simply amazing, and I can't wait to see what you do later on in life.

Anyway, I really appreciate you a whole lot. I hope to get to know you even better from here on out! Seriously. Don't be afraid to contact me at the below information. xo.

Sincerely,
Austin James Robinson

Theresa Deike,

If you're reading this, it's because you 'liked' or 'reacted' to a Facebook status I made back in April. I know, it's been awhile and I suck! I expect you to expect me to send you the Cheesecake Factory Menu or something – and honestly I will do that at a later time if you wish, – but this is a letter containing things I appreciate about you.

1). How personable you are and willing to make friends with anyone! I remember in APO when you were just willing to be friends with anyone in the organization. I know we were all like one big family, but you would go out of your way to talk to everyone! I thought that was really awesome.

2). That time you helped out my Student Government Executive Alliance campaign! You provided us with video content and constantly posted about our campaign on your social media. That was really awesome – I will forever be thankful for that! As you know, we were the smallest campaign, so that meant a lot to us.

3). Your dedication to the University of Texas. Even though you've graduated, you are apart of the medical staff for the football team, and that's amazing. You love and believe in the UT community so much that you went on to continue serving the campus even after graduating. Keep doing it!

Anyway, I really appreciate you a whole lot. I hope to get to know you even better from here on out! Seriously. Don't be afraid to contact me at the below information. xo.

Sincerely,
Austin James Robinson

[NAME REDACTED],

If you're reading this, it's because you 'liked' or 'reacted' to a Facebook status I made back in April. I know, it's been awhile and I suck! I expect you to expect me to send you the Cheesecake Factory Menu or something – and honestly I will do that at a later time if you wish, – but this is a letter containing things I appreciate about you.

1). Okay, so this is so embarrassing for me, but the only thing I know about you is that you live in [REDACTED] and that you're friends with all of my #[REDACTED]. So, of course I'm not going to sit here and stalk your Facebook and try to make up stuff to appreciate about you. Instead, I'll tell you about all of the times I've been ghosted. Are you ready?

2). Okay, so there was [REDACTED]. My first ever ghosting experience. He was a sophomore in college while I was a sophomore in high school, so there's no wonder there why he ghosted me. Then there was that guy who took me on a 16-hour date (literally) and then decided to ghost me the next day. I don't even know how that computes, but I gotta respect the emotional scam. Then there was my actual boyfriend, [REDACTED]. Idk why, but he decided to ghost me in the middle of us being together? That's some next level shit right there. Then this woman who works for a dating concierge service was all, "We're trying to showcase our service, so I'll be your personal dating concierge for free." Yeah, that never happened – she ghosted me! What the hell, my dating concierge ghosted me! Also, one time I had a prisoner pen-pal, and they eventually ghosted me, too. Anyway, what's up?

Anyway, I really appreciate you a whole lot. I hope to get to know you even better from here on out! Seriously. Don't be afraid to contact me at the below information. xo.

Sincerely,
Austin James Robinson

Tony Cummings,

If you're reading this, it's because you 'liked' or 'reacted' to a Facebook status I made back in April. I know, it's been awhile and I suck! I expect you to expect me to send you the Cheesecake Factory Menu or something – and honestly I will do that at a later time if you wish, – but this is a letter containing things I appreciate about you.

1). For being my Alpha Phi Omega little. I'm pretty sure you, Ryan, Jordan, and Christina are the weirdest pair to ever come out of APO, but also somehow y'all go perfectly together (how the hell did that even happen). We've had some good times in there. And, like, probably some bad times, too.

2). How basically anything that has ever been captured via camera in APO is because of you. There's really nothing else I can say about this – I don't remember the last time I saw a picture of an APO event that you didn't take.

3). The fact that I knew a Tony Cummings in high school and then you came along in college. That's pretty cool.

4). How your real name is Antonino and you pranked everyone into believing that your mother ACCIDENTALLY named you that instead of, like, Antonio. That was such a classic joke.

5). Remember when we both had the same exact "Summer Conference" bracelet from UT-Arlington because you were a worker there at the same time that I was apart of a conference? We probably met before we even knew each other (shocked face emoji).

Anyway, I really appreciate you a whole lot. I hope to get to know you even better from here on out! Seriously. Don't be afraid to contact me at the below information. xo.

Sincerely,
Austin James Robinson

Torii Carruth,

If you're reading this, it's because you 'liked' or 'reacted' to a Facebook status I made back in April. I know, it's been awhile and I suck! I expect you to expect me to send you the Cheesecake Factory Menu or something – and honestly I will do that at a later time if you wish, – but this is a letter containing things I appreciate about you.

1). How we used to practice tennis together and went to that tennis camp when we were, like, twelve-years-old. However, I didn't even really know who you were until I realized you were connected to Crystin Cox, who, at that time, really freaked me the fuck out. So, it's definitely a miracle that we're even here today.

2). The fact that you have a baby now. This is good because I really like babies, but I refuse to have one voluntarily until I'm, like, 40-years-old. So that leaves me with three options: 1). Find one in a dumpster. This shouldn't be that hard, but it may take a long time. I've already scoped out the dumpsters that are at higher risk of containing babies in my area. 2). Steal one from the fire station. Again, not hard, but still takes a lot of time to just stake out in front of a government building waiting for the perfect moment. Or, where you come in, 3). Become the godfather to a friend's baby and wait for their death. I already have a couple other friends who are also mothers, so this increases my chances of accidentally becoming a father. Thank you.

Anyway, I really appreciate you a whole lot. I hope to get to know you even better from here on out! Seriously. Don't be afraid to contact me at the below information. xo.

Sincerely,
Austin James Robinson

Travis Dudley,

If you're reading this, it's because you 'liked' or 'reacted' to a Facebook status I made back in April. I know, it's been awhile and I suck! I expect you to expect me to send you the Cheesecake Factory Menu or something – and honestly I will do that at a later time if you wish, – but this is a letter containing things I appreciate about you.

1). Hey! Okay, so I'm going to be completely honest here: I don't think we've really ever talked before. I mean, I know you had a dream about me once and messaged me about it, but that's the extent of our friendship. And I don't want to make up a bunch of bullshit to act like I know you and whatnot. So, I'm going to tell you a story:

2). You're from Brownwood, so I'm sure this will feel familiar to you. I remember going to church at Victory Life Academy one day. My friend wanted me to go and I guess I'm a good friend. Anyway, the pastor legitimately stated, "… and that's why gay people always die before the age of 45." He was talking about how being gay is a sin before all of that, and then he drops THAT bomb. Like, omg, I WISH we were guaranteed death at 45, am I right? But no, we have to live JUST AS LONG as straights! Kind of giving false hope here. Anyway, thanks for listening!

Anyway, I really appreciate you a whole lot. I hope to get to know you even better from here on out! Seriously. Don't be afraid to contact me at the below information. xo.

Sincerely,
Austin James Robinson

[NAME REDACTED],

If you're reading this, it's because you 'liked' or 'reacted' to a Facebook status I made back in April. I know, it's been awhile and I suck! I expect you to expect me to send you the Cheesecake Factory Menu or something – and honestly I will do that at a later time if you wish, – but this is a letter containing things I appreciate about you.

1). The fact that you didn't even like the status, but I'm sending you one of these anyway. Oh wait, this sounds like something I appreciate about myself. Oops.

2). How we matched on a dating app in ANCHORAGE and you just happened to know about my t-shirt brand, and then gave me a ride to the airport. That was a really great time and I don't even know how it all happened, but THANK YOU.

3). How we have a similar sense of humor. Well, at least when it comes to naughty emoji chain texts and conspiracy theories – which is truly all there is in the world. Thank you for putting up with all of my self-made comedy content.

4). How attractive you are. Yeah, idk, I told you this a million times back when you were single. Like, you are literally one of the most attractive people I have ever met in my life. And your personality is amazing. And God Damnit.

Anyway, I really appreciate you a whole lot. I hope to get to know you even better from here on out! Seriously. Don't be afraid to contact me at the below information. xo.

Sincerely,
Austin James Robinson

Trent Devon,

If you're reading this, it's because you 'liked' or 'reacted' to a Facebook status I made back in April. I know, it's been awhile and I suck! I expect you to expect me to send you the Cheesecake Factory Menu or something – and honestly I will do that at a later time if you wish, – but this is a letter containing things I appreciate about you.

1). Ayyy, Stinky Asshat! How are you? I honestly cannot remember when we first became friends. Like when or where or what. Was it the Skating Rink? It was probably the Skating Rink. Probably back in, like, middle school honestly. Who can never be sure? Regardless, we have been friends – or at least acquaintances / online BUDDIES – for years and years. That's kind of something special.

2). The time we played drunk hide-and-seek in the dark in your apartment and then Torii broke your bedroom window. Also, let me just say that hide-and-seek in the dark while playing mid-2000s Disney Channel Original Movie music is the creepiest thing I've ever done in my entire life. No wonder Torii broke your window – she was probably trying to get out of there.

3). How funny you and Torii are when you're together. Y'all create your own memes off of the top of y'all's heads all the time and they are fucking funny. Y'all really need to start putting them on the web!

Anyway, I really appreciate you a whole lot. I hope to get to know you even better from here on out! Seriously. Don't be afraid to contact me at the below information. xo.

Sincerely,
Austin James Robinson

Tristan Voss,

If you're reading this, it's because you 'liked' or 'reacted' to a Facebook status I made back in April. I know, it's been awhile and I suck! I expect you to expect me to send you the Cheesecake Factory Menu or something – and honestly I will do that at a later time if you wish, – but this is a letter containing things I appreciate about you.

1). How different you are. When you came to Brownwood, I'm pretty sure nobody was ready. You were easily the coolest person I met during my time at the high school. You seemed like such an unlikely Brownwood citizen – you made music, knew about underground things, and had this personality that immediately stood out among everyone. I'm really glad you got out of Brownwood, but I hope you're somewhere just as cool as you are where you are able to develop and follow your passion(s).

2). Your ability to befriend anyone and be liked by basically everyone. Idk, but I'm pretty sure you're rich. Like, I don't exactly remember if we ever discussed this, but I've always had this idea about you that your family is probably rich af. And that's cool, but I'm glad it doesn't make you feel as if you have to be apart of this superior class of people who refuse to talk to anyone lower than them. You're pretty much compatible with most people in my experience, and I think a lot of people like you for you simply being yourself opposed to what stereotypes are expected of you. That's dope af thooo.

Anyway, I really appreciate you a whole lot. I hope to get to know you even better from here on out! Seriously. Don't be afraid to contact me at the below information. xo.

Sincerely,
Austin James Robinson

Troy McDonald,

If you're reading this, it's because you 'liked' or 'reacted' to a Facebook status I made back in April. I know, it's been awhile and I suck! I expect you to expect me to send you the Cheesecake Factory Menu or something – and honestly I will do that at a later time if you wish, – but this is a letter containing things I appreciate about you.

1). The fact that we went to Hugh O'Brian Youth Leadership together! Wait, I think maybe you were the year after me. So maybe we didn't technically go through it together, but we've definitely volunteered at it together for years now. And I love when people come back to HOBY and continue year after year. You're going to have to come to one of the out-of-state seminars with me someday! I really only go to Alaska's now, but I'm literally down to go anywhere. Just tell me!

2). Your personality is, like, really great. It's no secret that everyone thinks you're incredibly nice and personable. I think you're always one of the favorite volunteers when we do HOBY every year. I'm so happy people like you exist in the world because I really hate mean people.

3). You're hot.

Anyway, I really appreciate you a whole lot. I hope to get to know you even better from here on out! Seriously. Don't be afraid to contact me at the below information. xo.

Sincerely,
Austin James Robinson

Tyler Corley,

If you're reading this, it's because you 'liked' or 'reacted' to a Facebook status I made back in April. I know, it's been awhile and I suck! I expect you to expect me to send you the Cheesecake Factory Menu or something – and honestly I will do that at a later time if you wish, – but this is a letter containing things I appreciate about you.

1). How I don't think we've ever met or seen each other in person before at all. Yet, somehow we're friends on Facebook and have messaged each other really dumb stuff. Amazing. Also, according to our message history, apparently we were supposed to go to a Sufjan Stevens concert together or something? I have no clue.

2). Your sense of humor. You've sent me naughty emoji chain texts before and you make really dumb songs for SoundCloud – both things that I do! Wow, how have we never met! Now that I'm thinking about it, I think we met through [REDACTED], who doesn't really talk to me anymore. So we may just never know. And that's what I've always loved about us.

3). How hot you are. I'm pretty sure I've told you that before. If not, here you go! I'm not sure what it is, but it's probably almost definitely just the fact that you're a Computer Scientist and I'm in love with that. I tried to join that LAN fraternity in Computer Science, but they rejected me (understandably – I was a Liberal Arts and Education major).

Anyway, I really appreciate you a whole lot. I hope to get to know you even better from here on out! Seriously. Don't be afraid to contact me at the below information. xo.

Sincerely,
Austin James Robinson

[NAME REDACTED],

If you're reading this, it's because you 'liked' or 'reacted' to a Facebook status I made back in April. I know, it's been awhile and I suck! I expect you to expect me to send you the Cheesecake Factory Menu or something – and honestly I will do that at a later time if you wish, – but this is a letter containing things I appreciate about you.

1). Your ability to chase your dreams. I think it's so fucking bad-ass that you're in a band and that you're making music. I know you truly love doing that and not a lot of people end up doing what they love, so this speaks volumes. I remember when we used to talk about [REDACTED] together and one time I wore your [REDACTED] sweatshirt at the [REDACTED]. I can't wait to hear the music you're making.

2). How kind and drama-free you are. Coming from [REDACTED], these character traits are quite rare. I really adore how kind you are to everyone you meet and how you aren't quick to judge anyone. Likewise, you don't engage or start anything that could be considered drama, which is cool because it probably means I'll never have a problem with our friendship lol.

3). Your name. Idk, this one is pretty self explanatory and I'm sure you get "omg I love your last name!" a lot, so excuse this obvious compliment.

Anyway, I really appreciate you a whole lot. I hope to get to know you even better from here on out! Seriously. Don't be afraid to contact me at the below information. xo.

Sincerely,
Austin James Robinson

[NAME REDACTED],

If you're reading this, it's because you 'liked' or 'reacted' to a Facebook status I made back in April. I know, it's been awhile and I suck! I expect you to expect me to send you the Cheesecake Factory Menu or something – and honestly I will do that at a later time if you wish, – but this is a letter containing things I appreciate about you.

1). We have the same middle name. This has to be the dumbest point I've written for any of my letters so far, but honestly you're better than everyone else solely because we have the same middle name.

2). How our friendship sparked because of someone else, but I feel like I've totally known you since before them for some reason. I fucking love your sense of humor and your thoughts. We have extremely similar opinions and view the world through a similar lens. I love that. It's always a pleasure getting to talk with you.

3). How cool you were that time I literally blew up your phone while I was black-out drunk and basically called you beautiful the entire time. I also kept crying and telling you that I was disrespecting your girlfriend, but that I wanted to be with you. What a time! But you were super cool about it the next day, and we're still good friends. Anyway, I can't wait to see you soon!

Anyway, I really appreciate you a whole lot. I hope to get to know you even better from here on out! Seriously. Don't be afraid to contact me at the below information. xo.

Sincerely,
Austin James Robinson

[NAME REDACTED],

If you're reading this, it's because you 'liked' or 'reacted' to a Facebook status I made back in April. I know, it's been awhile and I suck! I expect you to expect me to send you the Cheesecake Factory Menu or something – and honestly I will do that at a later time if you wish, – but this is a letter containing things I appreciate about you.

1). The fact that I'm pretty sure you were the first person ever to be interested in / to buy my t-shirt. It's funny enough that we both ended up at the same university together, let alone that you bought my shirt a hot several years before everyone else at the university did. You are truly the original fan / brand groupie. AMAZING. Thank you so much for your continued support.

2). The fact that you're an [REDACTED] and that we found a mutual friend in [REDACTED]. You know who (whom?) I'm talking about. [REDACTED]. AKA the reason we basically reunited. I can't believe we went on to join two organizations that are basically the same, and then have to deal with [REDACTED] (it's a blessing and a curse). I can't wait to see if we literally end up in the same things again in the future!

Anyway, I really appreciate you a whole lot. I hope to get to know you even better from here on out! Seriously. Don't be afraid to contact me at the below information. xo.

Sincerely,
Austin James Robinson

Varun Adiga,

If you're reading this, it's because you 'liked' or 'reacted' to a Facebook status I made back in April. I know, it's been awhile and I suck! I expect you to expect me to send you the Cheesecake Factory Menu or something – and honestly I will do that at a later time if you wish, – but this is a letter containing things I appreciate about you.

1). Your lovely and beautiful personality. Dude, you are always smiling and just as happy as can be. I love that. I absolutely love that. It brightens my day. Plus, you try to get to know people. I remember when we were leaving the Brave The Shave event at UT together and you just kept asking me questions about myself and my brand – and I could tell that you sincerely wanted to know. I'm sure you make so many people feel special <3

2). The fact that you wear crocs. I love crocs. I seriously love crocs. I'm so happy you wear them and aren't ASHAMED.

3). I want to get to know you better. I know this isn't something about you – it's just a fact that I want to state right now. I want to get to know you better, so I'll be messaging you soon. But if I forget, please reach out to me!!!!

Anyway, I really appreciate you a whole lot. I hope to get to know you even better from here on out! Seriously. Don't be afraid to contact me at the below information. xo.

Sincerely,
Austin James Robinson

[NAME REDACTED],

If you're reading this, it's because you 'liked' or 'reacted' to a Facebook status I made back in April. I know, it's been awhile and I suck! I expect you to expect me to send you the Cheesecake Factory Menu or something – and honestly I will do that at a later time if you wish, – but this is a letter containing things I appreciate about you.

1). You're in [REDACTED] with me. Yeah, I know – "What a dumb thing to appreciate about me!!" True – but also, not true. You being in [REDACTED] shows that you're an exemplary person who has so much to give to humanity and the world, in general. I cannot wait to see what you do one day as a [REDACTED].

2). That one time we went to the [REDACTED]. Do you remember that? That's when I bought that [REDACTED] t-shirt and we bought [REDACTED] for… honestly, I don't even remember who we bought [REDACTED] for. But also there was that woman who came up to us and was all, "Oh, I left my phone in my husband's car and he's not here yet. Can you text him?" And she literally had me text him, "Come get your wife." I still have that conversation saved.

Anyway, I really appreciate you a whole lot. I hope to get to know you even better from here on out! Seriously. Don't be afraid to contact me at the below information. xo.

Sincerely,
Austin James Robinson

Vincent Carson,

If you're reading this, it's because you 'liked' or 'reacted' to a Facebook status I made back in April. I know, it's been awhile and I suck! I expect you to expect me to send you the Cheesecake Factory Menu or something – and honestly I will do that at a later time if you wish, – but this is a letter containing things I appreciate about you.

1). THE FACT THAT WE BASICALLY GOT HALF MARRIED. I can't believe we literally met on a dating app and then that same night we agreed to get fake married. And within the same week, we were both at the Travis County Clerk's office asking them to marry us. We dressed up in nice clothes and everything. They totally thought we were going to actually get married. We fooled them! And then we actually bought the papers and got put in the governmental database saying we applied for marriage. I know you were there too, but I just have to say all of this out loud because it was so amazing. Then we got someone to take professional pictures of us and our new marriage certificate at a park. WHO ARE WE?

2). Okay and then we made a YouTube channel about being married and living in Hanover, New Hampshire and being candle hoarders, essentially. I can't believe we made, like, 20 different videos of us reviewing candles. What the hell are we going to do in the future?

3). Everything else. There is absolutely way too much to list about why I appreciate you, so I'm going to stop with the top two stories. But there is going to be so much more to come. I can't wait.

Anyway, I really appreciate you a whole lot. I hope to get to know you even better from here on out! Seriously. Don't be afraid to contact me at the below information. xo.

Sincerely,
Austin James Robinson

[NAME REDACTED],

If you're reading this, it's because you 'liked' or 'reacted' to a Facebook status I made back in April. I know, it's been awhile and I suck! I expect you to expect me to send you the Cheesecake Factory Menu or something – and honestly I will do that at a later time if you wish, – but this is a letter containing things I appreciate about you.

1). The fact that we have these weird periods in our lives where we're either best friends or we don't talk at all. It sounds kind of shitty, but I guess I cherish it this way regardless. Of course I absolutely adore when we talk every day and hang out and chat on the phone. But I feel like we maybe wear each other out too much to the point where we need to recharge. And although we're currently on low battery, I know we'll get back to the friendship soon.

2). Your love for [REDACTED] and education and leadership and service and ETC. You are so dedicated to changing the world, and also going to [REDACTED]. You have been there so many times, and I hope you get to go so many more times. I can't remember whether or not you've said you want to live there, but I hope your dreams come true – and I know they will. You are going to change the entire world.

3). The fact that I am in love with you and have been for a long time and will always be. I know that sounds really serious, but I don't mean it that way. However, I definitely don't mean it lightly. You know I've had a serious crush on you for years now. And I know you're not into me, but that doesn't mean I won't stop having a crush on you any time soon. And it's most definitely for the best that we don't date or anything – but I am still in love with all that you do and everything that makes you, you.

Anyway, I really appreciate you a whole lot. I hope to get to know you even better from here on out! Seriously. Don't be afraid to contact me at the below information. xo.

Sincerely,
Austin James Robinson

[NAME REDACTED],

If you're reading this, it's because you 'liked' or 'reacted' to a Facebook status I made back in April. I know, it's been awhile and I suck! I expect you to expect me to send you the Cheesecake Factory Menu or something – and honestly I will do that at a later time if you wish, – but this is a letter containing things I appreciate about you.

1). Your dedication to [REDACTED]. Or I guess your prior dedication now considering we are both graduated. You were one of the most known and active members in that organization – I really appreciate everything that you did to make that a worthwhile service opportunity for me. I was only in it for a year and a half, but I had some of the best times of my college career because of that organization. And a lot of that is because of the work you put into it.

2). The fact that we send naughty emoji chain texts to each other. You're one of those people who I know I can send a naughty emoji chain text to when I've made one or I've come across one. I haven't really been in the loop with them lately – and I haven't made one in forever – but I will definitely send them to you if I ever start making them again!

Anyway, I really appreciate you a whole lot. I hope to get to know you even better from here on out! Seriously. Don't be afraid to contact me at the below information. xo.

Sincerely,
Austin James Robinson

Zach Oltman,

If you're reading this, it's because you 'liked' or 'reacted' to a Facebook status I made back in April. I know, it's been awhile and I suck! I expect you to expect me to send you the Cheesecake Factory Menu or something – and honestly I will do that at a later time if you wish, – but this is a letter containing things I appreciate about you.

1). How you're one of the first people I ever talked to at the University of Texas. Literally my first semester we had that Psychology course together (the one I ended up Q-dropping at the last minute and then switching my major because of). And your first ever message to me was, "Yo man have you been studying for this exam???" Amazing. Then we sort of just kept following each other on social media because I think we're both pretty funny. Thank God I was a Psychology major for a hot minute, am I right!

2). You're hot af. Idk, I've just always thought you were hot. This is how you're finding out. Isn't that cool?

3). How, like, sort of bro-y you are but also completely chill and just like everyone else. Did that even make sense? Do I even know what I'm saying right now? Is this even a valid compliment that you're going to appreciate, or at this point have you already printed this out, ripped it up, and burned down the house?

Anyway, I really appreciate you a whole lot. I hope to get to know you even better from here on out! Seriously. Don't be afraid to contact me at the below information. xo.

Sincerely,
Austin James Robinson

Z

What did I learn? Well, first and foremost, I learned not to joke around. Like, literally I need to reevaluate my comedy style because I am definitely likely to get myself into a 100-hour-long project again simply by posting a status on Facebook. But more importantly, I assessed and evaluated my friendship with 217 people – people I have known from childhood to just a couple months ago. I expressed my appreciation for them not only to myself throughout the process, but also to these individuals through these letters. I gained a deeper understanding of what friendship means to me and what each and every one of these friends has contributed to that understanding. My passion for treating the people in my life as celebrities and stars has only deepened and rooted itself in my life. Now, I'm not about to make a t-shirt with each and every person's name on it – that would cost entirely too much. However, I can document my appreciation for my friends such as I am doing right now. I can let it be known that I care for them and am willing to go out of my way to ensure they feel loved and valued. I can spread this activity to others and hope for a movement where we treasure the people in our lives and actively think about friendship opposed to simply allowing it to be a passive act in our lives.

More specifically, I learned that I have friends from all over the world. I sent these letters to people from several different countries, backgrounds, and lifestyles. Granted, most of these people are from the University of Texas at Austin, and most of them were involved in a service organization I had ties to. However, I was still surprised to learn that my friends are widely spread out and have experiences vastly different than my own. I began to appreciate the differences I have with my friends, because they allow me to access a worldview that I wouldn't otherwise have without our friendship. Although I do enjoy when me and a friend are similar and can relate on a variety of levels, I believe it is of the utmost importance to not only befriend those who may come from a background that is a bit uncomfortable to you, but also utilize their experience and knowledge to help yourself grow as a human being. And that's not a one-way street – I can guarantee that if you are growing due to someone's understanding of life, then they are also growing from yours. Lessons learned don't always have to be intrapersonal – they can be interpersonal, too. Or better yet, they can be expressed via letters of appreciation. Also, I have way too many friends named Christopher.

And finally, I learned that I have some kick-ass friends. They have done incredible things, from producing music to being international Cheerleaders to biking 4,000 miles to Alaska, and then some. They have gone on Study Abroad with me, created Canadian plays / musicals, and established meaningful (and meme-ingful) organizations at universities. They sing in bands, juggle on their free time, and advocate for underprivileged communities. My friends have had intense and life-changing experiences that I may not personally completely understand, but can learn from simply by calling them my friend. I even "married" one of them!

NOW IT'S YOUR TURN

So, here's your homework. I want you to do as I did and write letters to over 200 people. I'm kidding – I want you to simply write a letter to at least one person regarding what you appreciate about them. I have included five templates for you. They are similar to how I structured my letters. Copy and paste it over to your computer and send away. Or rip the pages out of this book and mail them. I don't even care if you fill them out and then mail the entire book to a person's physical location. Just tell your friends how much you appreciate them.

PROJECT LETTERS

Dear _____,

_____
_____
_____
_____

1). _____
_____
_____
_____
_____
_____
_____
_____

2). _____
_____
_____
_____
_____
_____
_____
_____

3). _____
_____
_____
_____
_____
_____
_____
_____
_____

Sincerely,

_____

PROJECT LETTERS

Dear _____,

_____
_____
_____
_____

1)._____
_____
_____
_____
_____
_____
_____
_____

2)._____
_____
_____
_____
_____
_____
_____
_____

3)._____
_____
_____
_____
_____
_____
_____
_____
_____
_____

Sincerely,

_____

PROJECT LETTERS

Dear _____,

_____
_____
_____

1)._____
_____
_____
_____
_____
_____

2)._____
_____
_____
_____
_____
_____

3)._____
_____
_____
_____
_____
_____
_____

Sincerely,

_____

PROJECT LETTERS

Dear _____,

_____
_____
_____

1)._____
_____
_____
_____
_____
_____

2)._____
_____
_____
_____
_____
_____

3)._____
_____
_____
_____
_____
_____
_____

                                Sincerely,

                              _____

PROJECT LETTERS

Dear _____,

_____
_____
_____
_____

1)._____
_____
_____
_____
_____
_____
_____

2)._____
_____
_____
_____
_____
_____
_____

3)._____
_____
_____
_____
_____
_____
_____
_____
_____

                                           Sincerely,

                                     _____

ABOUT THE AUTHOR

www.austinjamesrobinson.org

www.ingramcontent.com/pod-product-compliance
Lightning Source LLC
Chambersburg PA
CBHW060316050426
42449CB00011B/2503